The Way Things Were

Short Stories of Past Experiences

By

Robert J. Walker (Bobby)

"Enjoy Reading"

Robert Walker

863. 3809823

(Comments Appreciated)

ISBN: 1-4033-8227-1 (e-book)
ISBN: 1-4033-8228-X (Paperback)

This book is printed on acid free paper.

1stBooks – rev. 11/27/02

DEDICATION

to My Children and Grandchildren

A special note to my children, grandchildren, great grandchildren, my nieces, and nephews, and all of the Walker generations to come!

The Way Things Were is a collection of short stories that I have written in order to help preserve the memory and history of a way of life that once existed in the 1900's (Twentieth Century). It was a time in the late 1940's and early 1950's when we, Charles (Billy), Robert (Bobby), and Elaine (Chicken) were children growing up in Sebring, Florida and Millen, Georgia.

I think the Walkers of the 2000's must have some information regarding the Walker's of the 1900's. I also want the future generations to know the principles and what it was like when I was a child: the atmosphere of the 1900's, the people and racial issues; nature and climate, animal and plant life; the working and living conditions of Black People; the economic and political situations of that time, and of course the conditions on the Home Farm of Grandpa, Alfred Walker, in Millen, Georga.

Grandpa's daddy was Willis Walker and his wife's name was Bessie. Great Grandpa lived in Waynesburg, Georgia. Willis and Bessie had seven children: Alfred, Rosy, Charlie, Aaron, Marian, Sadie and Catherine.

Grandma Louise had twelve brothers and sisters: Bessie, Mary, Sadie, Lillie, Flora, Ella, Willie, Johnny, Sam, Lee, James, and Nathaniel. Modfett was Grandma Louise's maiden name, and she was born in Waynesburg, Georgia Grandpa (Alfred Walker), born June 16, 1871 in Waynesburg, Georgia, moved to Millen, Georgia in 1916 when Daddy (Charlie Walker) was five years old. That was the year that Uncle Albert accidentally hit Daddy on the head with an axe while cutting wood.

Grandpa (Alfred Walker) had ten children by two wives, Mary and Louise: Ezekiel, Hattie, Nellie, James and Lila; Johnny, Albert, Charlie, Willis, and Louise. (Charlie, my daddy, was born May 16, 1911.)

In 1926-27 Grandpa Alfred bought the Walker's farm land in Millen, Georgia, where he grew cotton on fifty-seven acres of land. Cotton was the money-producing crop at that time.

Grandpa Alfred had three mules, two horses, several carriages, seventeen milk cows with calves, four bulls, hundreds of hogs and pigs, chickens and ducks.

Grandpa Alfred and his wives, Mary and Louise, and much later Susie, also grew gardens to produce their vegetables: beans, peas, collards and mustard greens, carrots, etc. Fruit trees were all over the property, such as pecans, apples, pears, plums, walnuts, peaches, grapes and blue and black berries, pumpkins, water melons and peanuts.

Grandpa and his wives actually lived off the land and their own farm animals. The cows provided milk from which Grandma would make butter, and cream; and from the cows came steaks and all the parts of the beef meat family. The hogs provided all the pork meat family, such as sausages, chitlings, bacon, and pork chops just to name a few.

Grandma would make syrup and sugar from the cane crop and from the fruits she would make jelly's, jams, and wine.

The smoke or cold house was the place for storing meats, milk, jellies, jams, wine or any foods that were to be kept for a period of time. The smoke house was a cellar dug into the ground or up against a red clay mound. The red clay kept the temperature in the room at a constant coolness…60 to 68 degrees.

Just about any medicine could be found in the nearby woods and fields if not actually growing on the farm, therefore very few people went to a doctor.

Both Grandpa Alfred and Grandma Susie used plants, roots and certain tree leaves as medicine. They knew which plants to dig up or leaves to pull or cut off a tree, boil, cook or use raw. They knew when, how much and how to apply these plants as medicine. Unfortunately, these secret techniques have gone to the grave with them.

Grandpa had a water well which was fed by a spring that never ran dry. That spring continues to run through the property in Millen, Georgia today, 2000...and it's the freshest, sweetest, water I have ever tasted.

Grandpa, Alfred Walker, outlived three wives. He farmed and worked until he was well into his nineties. Grandpa moved to Sebring, Florida to live with Daddy, Charlie Walker, in 1968. He died in his sleep after a healthy meal and evening walk around the neighborhood. He was ninety-nine at his death in 1970.

The information and history of Grandpa, Alfred Walker, and Charlie and Anna bell Walker is much too valuable to be lost and forgotten by the passing of time and the passing of those few relatives who lived in those wonderful, precious years when The Way Things Were was so different.

Minister Robert J. Walker

CONTENTS

1. Mother and Dad Jump the Broom 1

2. My First Spanking 6

3. Always On The Move 12

4. Home Sweet Home 19

5. The Colored School 23

6. First Visit To The Walker Farm 30

7. Blackie 39

8. Musical Raindrops 49

9. Hi Yo Silver 55

10. The Church Day in Millen, Georgia 66

11. A Colored Band In The Christmas Parade 72

12. A Summer To Remember 82

13. The Bike Ride 92

14. A Friend Called Junior 106

15. Mother Goes To College 115

16. Falsely Accused 120

17. The Price of Disobedience 125

18. A Real Man Is A Responsible Man 145

INTRODUCTION

In Memory of Charlie and Anna Bell Walker

One summer night in 1987 my mother Anna Bell Walker and I were talking about how things were when I was a little boy in Sebring, Florida. She and I laughed and rejoiced in the memories of days gone by of a time that would be no more.

We remembered and spoke of places, people and situations that had faded in history, and would soon be forgotten; a time and type of life that was vastly different from the present.

We spoke of her hometown...Macon, Georgia, where she attended school and later after marriage returned and thereby I was born in Macon.

Mother spoke about how she and my father (Charlie Walker) had met and married. She explained how she and Dad had a vision and how with prayer and faith they set out to accomplish and make that vision a reality.

Mother and I sat up that night talking about Millen, Georgia, and Grandpa and Grandma Walker on my daddy's side of the family. We talked about "the farm life" and how she made sure that her children (my brother Billy, sister Elaine and I, Bobby) were exposed to the farm by visiting Grandpa every summer after school.

During the summer of 1987 Mother stayed with me for several weeks, therefore we had many opportunities to talk about the way things were in the years gone by…

We talked about rare relationships and how we grew up in Sebring, Florida. It was a highly segregated city with "white town" on the west side of the Seaboard and Atlantic Coastline railroad tracks, which ran north and south, and the "Colored Town" on the east side of the railroad tracks. Colored Town was also called "Coon Town", "Boot Town", "Nigger Town", "Hodgemoore Quarters" or "The Quarters".

We talked of a time and place and a type of people who enjoyed some good situations, endured some terrible situations, were indifferent to a few situations, and tolerated many situations.

It was a time when Black People were ashamed to be called "Black" disliked being called "Colored" and hated being called a "nigger". It was a time when Black People gave reverence to GOD, even if some didn't worship or praise Him. They respected Him and prayer was as common as syrup in every colored person's home.

It was a time when fifty cents or one dollar an hour was common wages for a "colored man"; when white people didn't allow colored folks to ride in the front seat, therefore they chauffeured colored folks to and from work in their homes as maids, butlers, baby sitters, cooks, yard workers, etc.

As Mother and I talked into the early hours in the morning, it occurred to me that many of these things and situations we were discussing would be lost to my children, grand children, and great grand children unless I wrote down past occurrences in a diary or book.

Minister Robert J. Walker

Chapter 1

Mother and Dad Jump the Broom

I always did like the story of how my parents got together and one night during that summer of 1987 my mother stayed up most of the night telling me the story.

Let's see, my mother, whose name is Anna Belle but was called "Bee" by my dad, was about sixteen years old when she stepped off that train in Millen, Georgia in 1936. She was about five-feet four-inches tall, high yellow complexion, with long black hair hanging down about midway of her back. She wore a yellow dress with small red flowers. She shaded her face with a small yellow parasol, took her suitcase from the conductor and started walking toward the "colored" waiting room at the train station.

As she got off the train she saw three young colored men sitting near the waiting room on a baggage cart. Two of the young men jumped off the cart, pushing and shoving each other as they clumsily offered their assistance.

1

"Hey, Miss Fine Brown", then "let me hope you tote that bag". Tom was tall and light skinned, and he was usually the one who attracted the most attention from the girls.

"Miss, ya'll want me to hope you get somewhere?" asked Johnny. He was the shorter one of the three men and she noticed a slight limp as he walked, but he did have a nice smile with "near-perfect" white teeth.

BUT, it was the tall dark-skinned fellow that caught Bee's eye. He just stood there looking at her for a few moments, then he casually walked over and took her suitcase from her hand and said, "You're the new school teacher, ain't you? My name is Charlie and my car is right over here, I'll take you to Mrs. Summer's house, that's where you supposed to stay, ain't it?"

Bee blushed and nodded, "Yes" and was speechless for the entire ride to her rooming house; she was nervous, but yet excited by this tall, dark, handsome young man. She knew immediately that she would be seeing a whole lot more of this confident, dark-black man.

For the next few months, Charlie was escorting Bee to every social gathering in town. He escorted her to church as well, and helped her to become familiar with the countryside. He introduced her to the city folks and to many of the parents of the children whom she taught.

Mother said it wasn't long before she and Dad started talking about marriage. Mother was teaching school in the city and Dad was trying to make a living on a small thirty-five acre farm, but times were hard and cotton wasn't doing so good. But they were in love and wanted to be together.

Dad's parents, Grandpa and Grandma Louise Walker were happy for them and began to help and to plan for the wedding. Mother didn't know much about cooking. She was raised in the city and her mother, Ethel Jackson, (we called her "Good Mother") didn't teach her to cook. In fact, Mother was raised with the idea she was to marry a rich doctor or lawyer, certainly not a farmer.

In my case, Grandma Louise Walker told Mother that she had better learn to cook before she starts talking about marrying, so for two to three months Mother stayed around Grandma Louise's kitchen learning how to cook collard greens and black-eyed peas, also to fry chicken and to make cracklin' bread.

"Goodmother" didn't like this arrangement at all and tried her best to break off the engagement, but Mother and Dad were persistent and on February 30, 1936 Charlie and Anna Belle "Jumped The Broom".

Mother started teaching high school in Scarburgh, Georgia. It was a little place out in the country about six miles from the little farm that Dad owned and near Grandpa Alfred's large farm. Mother did not teach children during this time, she said, because the government paid more money for teaching adult education.

Mother said that she walked to and from that little one-room school where she taught first grade through nineth grade to about thirty adults.

Only a very few adult men were doing junior high school work and none were working in the high school level.

The school was also the church building where church services were held on Sunday and school was taught Monday through Friday. The building was also the meeting hall for the Masonic Lodge members on Saturday.

Dad worked the farm from sunup to sundown Monday through Saturday. Usually he worked only a half-day on Saturday and attended church on Sunday. Dad grew cotton and soybeans (the money crops) and corn, peanuts as back-up crops.

Grandma Louise taught Mother how to plant two large produce gardens. She taught Mother how to grow collard greens, mustard greens, peas, beans, tomatoes, cucumbers, carrots and watermelons. Since Grandpa Alfred's farm was near Mother and Dad's farm they shared fruit trees including pears, apples, plums, pecans, and walnuts along with grapes, and blue/black berries.

The first year of marriage was rough going for Dad and Mother, but they were happy and determined to make their life together a success. The next year my brother, Charles (Billy) was born January 4, 1937.

This was their beginning and the beginning of *The Way Things Were*.

Chapter 2
My First Spanking

This story takes place in a farm country on the outskirts of Macon, Georgia. They tell me that I was born in Macon, Georgia, August 7, 1938.

I've heard it said that it's impossible for a person to remember when they were younger than two years of age...Well, I don't know about that, you see, I can remember a spanking I received when I was a child about two or three years old.

At the time of this story, my mother was visiting with her cousin, Odessa who lived in Macon, Georgia. Odessa was a pretty lady about twenty years old. I knew what was pretty and what was ugly even at two years of age. And boy, Odessa was a good-looking lady just like Mother.

They called light-skinned colored people "high yellow" back in the 1940's and 1950's and Odessa was high yellow.

Anyway, Odessa lived on this little farm with her two daughters, Gertrude and Viola. "Mutt" and "Rat" was what we called them. It was years later when I was in my early twenties before I knew the real names of those two girls. Mutt was Gertrude and Rat was Viola.

There were a few farm animals on the little farm, plenty enough to excite my little two-year old mind. The house was built high off the ground like most farm houses in the country were built during those years (1930's through World War II until the late 1950's).

Later in Florida, when I explained this particular event to my mother, she told me I was nearly two years of age when this spanking occurred.

I remember on that day I was under the house playing with the "doodle" bugs, spiders and any other insects that looked interesting and remained close enough to me for me to grab and inspect. I can't remember what led me to be underneath the house; maybe it was the "dirt dabber", who is cousin to the wasp but doesn't sting. (I don't' think I knew that at the time).

I might have been fascinated with the way they flew to the little stream of water that was dripping under the back porch. The drip was coming from a small pipe that was connected to a sink on the back porch. Next to the sink was a water bucket and a dipper which was like a wash stand…a place to wash your hands and face before coming inside the main house.

People were real clean back in those days. They even had a special rug and a small brush, which was used to clean the bottom of your shoes after you've been walking around in the backyard. You see the backyard was the bathroom for chickens, ducks, and any other animal that cared to use it.

Oh, well, I was watching those "dirt dabbers" rolling the mud from the "drip stream", putting it in their mouths and flying under the house. I wanted to see what those insects were up to. After all, I didn't have anything urgent to do.

I had just had my bath, and my mother had put these real stiff clothes on me. My short collar was all buttoned up to the top and those hard sole shoes were hurting my feet. So to help forget my pain and misery, I decided I would just follow the next "Dabber" to see what they were doing with all that mud.

I crawled under that house and a whole new world was before me. The wonders that my two-year old eyes beheld, even "Alice In Wonderland" doesn't compare...Disney World is dull city.

There was activity everywhere and all around me...little creatures, big creatures, crawling bugs, flying insects, bugs, beetles, worms, a hog with piglets had found a nice cool corner, chickens with baby chicks, spiders and doodle bugs.

I found a nice cool spot and sat down to watch the "dirt dabber". He was building a hut on a nearby floorboard beam. I watched him flying back and forth, but soon began to notice the sand moving between my legs. The sand continued to move and soon a depression took place. I stuck my finger in the middle of the depression and discovered a small funny looking bug; later, I learned that the bug was called a "doodle bug".

As I look back to that day, I am reminded that all country farmhouses built with the space underneath had its own little world. Those little worlds are gone now; not many houses are built that way anymore. Underneath that house, I forgot my tight shoes and hot starched shirt...I was just having fun.

Then, I heard my mother calling, "Bobby, Bobby, where are you? Bobby, come on, it's time to go. Bobby, I know you're not under that house, not with your Sunday clothes on." Well, yes, I was under the house. I didn't understand what she meant by "Sunday clothes," but it was something in her voice that let me know that I was in trouble.

"Come on, come on from under there. You're gonna git it, Little Man! I told you not to get dirty". The words "Little Man" confirmed my deepest fear. I was in trouble. I mean "spanking" trouble!

When I came from under the house, my pretty white short pants and jacket were rather dirty. I guess the spider webs and red clay didn't make mother very happy.

She had a switch (a branch from a small peach tree) and was coming toward me. Then, I made one of the biggest mistakes of my life. I ran. I learned later that I was only about two-years old and at the time I thought running was a pretty darn good decision. But, I was wrong, mother outran me and caught me at the bottom of the slope of the backyard.

Mother proceeded to spank my little legs and butt all the way back up that hill into the house, into the bedroom…I never ran from my mother again, "yep," I got plenty of spankings. "But, I never ran again."

"That's the way things were."

Chapter 3

Always On The Move

"Bobby! Bobby! Come back inside before you fall down those stairs", my mother called to me again. I was standing at the top of the back stairs, looking down at the two little pretty yellow girls who were sitting on the bottom step.

I would like to go down and play with them, but before I could manage to get my little legs moving, Mother grabbed me and took me back inside the screen door, back to our small apartment which we rented from Mr. and Mrs. Bossie Watson.

I remember the green steps of the back stairs leading down to Lemon Street and the white sidewalk which led into my favorite spot, the Watson's Café.

In addition to the rooming house Mr. and Mrs. Bossy Watson owned and operated the restaurant. Mrs. Tresa Watson was a tremendous cook and many of the prominent Negroes came to eat at her café, not only on Saturday and Sunday, but also through the week. Most customers favored her big breakfasts. Not me. I wasn't interested in breakfast at the age of three and four. What I liked most was the ice cream parlor, which was in the back of the café. That was the place where I liked to visit all day.

I really did miss that ice cream parlor when we moved to another house for rent. In fact, we did a whole lot of moving from house to house in those early days.

My dad was trying to find a place for us in this city called Sebring, which was located in Central Florida, about ninety miles south of Tampa and one hundred-fifty miles north of Miami, Florida.

Dad's primary job at that time was the kind of labor most men found in Sebring and the surrounding cities, which was "picking fruit". (oranges and grapefruit) From what I was told, Daddy was one of the best fruit pickers in the country and could pick one hundred boxes of fruit a day, which was the best expected.

Dad made above average income in those days ($100.00 per week), but housing was just hard to come by. Since Dad and Mother had recently moved to Florida, they had to rent from other Negroes who had lived in the city long enough to have built a house. However, not many people wanted to rent a room to a couple with two very, very active boys.

Which brings us to Tees (Aunt Lillie Moore). As children, we couldn't pronounce Aunty, so we shortened it to "Tee" and then "Tees", which is what we children called her until her death.

Tees had been living in Sebring for several years…ever since she left the farm in Millen, Georgia. She had married and built a home on Booker Street.

She got tired of Daddy (her brother) moving us from place to place so she had an extra room added and moved us into her home. That arrangement was nice but still crowded.

Daddy also worked at Henry's Beer Saloon on Lemon Street during the evening and Mother worked and sang at the USO on Lemon Street. I remember one summer when my brother, Billy, was six years old. I was four years old and my sister, Elaine, was two years old.

I remember one Saturday afternoon when Tees had just come home from the orange grove. I knew it was Saturday because, first, I didn't have to go to the baby sitter and all morning I had been playing with Tee's dog, Spot. Spot and

I had been out in the back yard chasing the chickens. In those days it was not against the law to have chickens, ducks and hogs in your back yard around the house.

Secondly, Tees only worked a half day and also daddy would be coming home soon because nobody picked fruit the whole day on Saturday.

On Saturday, folks got paid, got groceries, got haircuts, and got their hair "done", would go to town, go to pay bills, go fishing, get bathed (full bath), get dressed, (I mean clean, sharp, dressed down), go to Lemon Street to get drunk, to dance, to party, to have fun and a good time.

Tees came in from work and sat down in her favorite rocking chair. "Billy is my water ready?" she asked. "Yes, um," my brother replied, as he came onto the front porch with the foot-tub of hot water, followed with the towel, knife and clippers. Tees would soak her feet in the hot water, then take the knife to scrap her feet of dead skin and then clip her toenails.

This was a normal routine each Saturday for Tee to clean her feet in this manner; and, we children looked forward to this ritual each Saturday. I was fascinated with all the dead skin she would peel off her feet with that sharp knife and she wouldn't bleed. (This was also my introduction to "toe jam".)

On this particular Saturday evening, all the adults in the house were going out for the evening. Mother was the hostess and featured singer at the USO Club for Negroes. Since the war was going-on, there were hundreds of Negro soldiers at the Sebring Air Base (Hendricks Field), who would come to town on the weekend. They were looking to have fun dancing, drinking, and spending a whole lot of money "juking". (Juking was a Negro term used to describe an evening out dancing, drinking, eating, and having fun.)

Dad was working at the Beer Saloon, Tees and Uncle Bill were going juking. An older boy called John, who lived across the street was to baby sit. But after we had taken our baths and were preparing for bed, we discovered that John had forgotten to put our pajamas out on the bed.

I knew where they were kept in the top drawer of the dresser in our bedroom. I was a short little guy, but determined to get my own pajamas; therefore, I pulled the bottom drawer out and stood on it, in order to reach the top drawer.

I could not and did not imagine my little body being heavy enough to topple that dresser, but it did happen along with the kerosene lamp that was on top of the dresser. The lamp fell to the floor. Kerosene spilled on the floor and the bed. The fire caught on the bed, I remember pulling the bedspread off the bed.

"Fire! Help! Help, Billy! Help Brother John!" Billy ran and got some water. Brother John stamped on the fire.

We were scared, but thank God we did not panic. We kids put that fire out, we didn't panic. We cleaned up the mess the fire made. We even opened the windows to allow fresh air to blow in and get rid of the smoky smell. Then we went to sleep like perfect little lambs.

The next afternoon (Sunday) Tees was outside feeding the chickens when she saw a burnt rag (tablecloth that was on the top of the dresser) in the outside trash barrel. She found other evidence, which she brought to Mother's and Dad's attention, who in turn questioned Bill and me. We told the truth about what had happened.

I think that it was at this point that Dad decided he must get his own home and not have us kids destroying his sister's place. But that's another adventure and story in *The Way Things Were*.

Chapter 4

Home Sweet Home

We had been living with Aunt Tees in Sebring, Florida for sometime now. Billy and I had almost set Tees's house on fire, so Daddy decided to build his family "a home".

Dad had us up early this particular morning and told us to get on the back of the truck, "We are going to work".

The night before at supper while sitting around the table, Daddy had said he had a job for us boys to do the next day, and then he sent us to bed. Therefore, Billy and I had no idea what job we were to do. I didn't care what it was, I was excited to finally work. I mean real work, not house or yard work; and to my little five-year-old mind, I was gonna do a man's job. I was so happy and excited.

So here it was the next morning and we were on the back of Mr. Jacksonville's truck, riding out in the countryside. We passed many orange groves and pretty soon we were out in an open pasture. I could see a few cows and horses out in the distance. Dust was flying up and it was starting

19

to get hot as the sun got higher in the sky, but Billy and I were laughing and having fun just being on this bumpy ride, "on our way to work."

Daddy finally said, "Here we are boys." I looked up to see this old big house that looked like it had been struck by lightening.

Daddy and Mr. Jacksonville stood looking at it for a moment then Mr. Jacksonville said, "Well, Charlie, let's get with it! It ain't going to move by itself." And then, they began to get the equipment and tools. (hammers, saws, crowbars, etc.)

"Billy, you're to pull all those old boards over here to the shade. And, you Bobby, take this hammer, pull out all those nails; and, Bobby, come here, let me show you what else I want you to do!"

"This is your special job, little man!" (How about that, I was gonna have my special job. Boy, did I feel proud!)

Dad showed me how to take a nail out of a board then place the nail on a brick; then he would straighten out the bent nail by hitting it until it was almost straight as new. That was my job! To straighten out the old nails, and place them in a jar. We were saving the nails to use again when Dad built our new home. The nails that were too old or crooked I would throw away.

I don't know how many times we made that trip to the cow pasture to tear down that old house, but we took that house down piece by piece, board by board...roof, floor, sides, etc. Every part of that house, including the front and back porches, that wasn't damaged, we loaded Mr. Jacksonville's truck and took it to 320 Harris Street. (later named 704 Zion Street)

That address is where Dad built the house for his family and I can't remember how long it took him to build that house. He did most of the work himself except for the electrical work and some of the plumbing, which was done by Mr. Preston Cain and Reverend Harris.

I do know that I was five-years old the day that we started tearing down the old house in the cow pasture and I was six-years old in the first grade, when we moved into the new house in 1945. I remember my first day going to school, because our new home was directly across from the

Negro school (E. O. Douglas) which was first grade through twelfth grade.

We had our own house! Billy and I had our own bedroom with our own bed. We slept together the first year. Elaine had her own bedroom and Mother and Dad had their own bedroom.

It was a dream house with three bedrooms, a kitchen, bathroom, dining room, a front porch with four huge red brick pillars to hold up the roof, a back porch, a huge fireplace and a wood bin for firewood. Daddy later built a carport and washhouse (a place to wash clothes) for Mother.

The Walkers finally had a home…no more moving from house to house!

Thank God, thank Dad and Mother, for that was "The Way Things Were" in 1944-45.

Chapter 5

The Colored School

The summer of 1944 was a busy time, an exciting time, a scary time and a fun time, all mixed together.

Our family had just moved into a new home that my Dad had built, directly across from the Negro school, E. O. Douglas. It consisted of grades one through twelve and offered the first Negro high school in Sebring. The building was named for Mr. E. O. Douglas, bank president, who was a very civic-minded citizen of Sebring.

The main school building was a huge magnificent building to my five-year, eleven-month old mind. It was the biggest building in my whole wide world.

The front of the building faced east with a huge front lawn and eight Royal Palm trees. Four trees on each side of the long sidewalk leading down from Highlands Avenue to the double front door of the school.

Once inside past the double doors, there was a long, long hallway with offices and classrooms on each side. The principal's office was the first office on the right. The second door led to the social studies class and the third door to the Home Makers of America class taught by Mrs. Robinson. The junior and senior high school girls learned how to cook, sew and clean house. They were taught proper table manners and how to set the table for meals, how to dress and match their clothes colors.

During this time period before integration, Negroes believed in teaching their children how to take care of a home and take care of themselves; not like it is today when some mothers don't bother to teach their daughters how to cook and sew, or how to comb and style their hair, etc.

The reason I remember so much about NHA (New Home Makers of America) is that many years later when I would reach 11th grade I had to take a semester of NHA.

Back to the school building…on the left side of the long hallway were other class rooms, but at the very end was another double door, which opened into an all-purpose room. This huge room was the auditorium, the assembly room, the junior-senior prom room, the drama room, the skating room, the ballroom and the PTA meeting room.

On the outside of the main building were barracks, which were brought in from the old Sebring Air Base (Hendricks Field). These barracks were used for classrooms one through six grades. There were two classes in each barrack. Also there was one very long barrack which was the lunchroom and kitchen.

These barracks were to the rear of the main building. The primary and elementary schools formed a half moon circle. The first barrack on the northwest side was for the first and second grades and the next barrack was for third and fourth grades. The next barrack was for the fifth and sixth grade. The main building was off limits to primary and elementary kids.

You had to be a "big kid" to even go into the main hallway, except when you had "got into trouble" and had to go see the principal. (I got to see the main hallway a whole lot while I was in school.)

Oh, yea! I don't want to forget the clay basketball court. I mean red clay…watered down and packed hard with a 300 pound roller then lined with white lime according to SIAC basketball regulations and measurements.

Robert J. Walker (Bobby)

Mr. Hart was the assistant principal and basketball coach. I remember helping him prepare the basketball court for basketball games. I would also help him with the balls/equipment. Later at some point he made me "ball/equipment boy" and I traveled with the team to all of the games. Mr. Hart was my primary "mentor" in sports. He was the person who inspired and motivated me in sports. Because of him, I became "All Conference Athlete" in basketball and football, which made it possible for me to get an Athletic Scholarship to Tuskegee University in 1958.

A ten-foot wooden fence was built around the basketball court during basketball season to keep out non-paying spectators. In each corner was a large sized barrel. The men would start a fire in the barrels to provide warmth during cool winter basketball games.

The summer that I turned six years old on August 7, 1944, my older brother, Billy said, "Bobby next month you're going to school." Well I had been in kindergarten with Mrs. Jannie Green and I had been told that kindergarten was a little like school...You played, read

26

stories, took a nap, played some more, had lunch, took another nap, had snacks, and played some more. So what was the big deal? The school was across from our house, which meant I didn't have to walk all the way up to Lemon Street where the kindergarten school was located. So "bring on the school", I thought. I was ready!

School Day

I don't remember waking up that morning, I don't remember dressing, saying my blessing, eating breakfast, making up my bed or even going to the bathroom to brush my teeth. But I suppose I did those things because it was a normal routine each morning. I don't remember Daddy saying "have a good first day at school, big man", or Mother hugging me and saying "You be a very good boy and tell Mrs. Mason hello!"

You see, I was so excited that I don't remember any of that; but I am sure that's what my parents did. What I do remember is Billy taking me by the hand and walking with me to that first barracks…first grade and Mrs. Mason.

Billy opened the door, pushed me in the door and said, "You're here now, I gotta go, bye." And left me…all alone…standing there in that doorway looking into that roommmmmmm.

Little black, brown and yellow children were every where. Some were crying, some were sitting on benches or on the floor; some were trying to climb out the windows. I think one or two did manage to get out the door when we came in. Some were hugging their mother's legs, holding on to their dresses, pocket books, ankles, and anything on their mother's body to keep her from leaving them. Some crying out, "Mama, mama, I don't wanna stay…Mama, you comin' backs?"

I stood there looking and listening; trying to understand where in the world did all these little kids come from. I thought I knew everybody, especially the little children like me. I saw Robert B., Simon C., Albert M., Richard B., Gerture R., Jean J., Charlotte R., and Joyce. J. I knew these kids, we were in kindergarten. But who were these other strange kids? Some were running around the room crying, yelling, screaming and pushing and shoving one another. I didn't understand why these kids were crying. Why were some of them looking so afraid?

Being Daddy's "Big Man", I took a seat near the door and waited for Mrs. Mason to finish talking with several parents who were attempting to disengage themselves from their clinging children.

Soon, I saw Mrs. Mason pick up a long ruler from the blackboard. Tap it on her desk three times and she said, "Children Be Quiet, please"…so my school education began.

More to come about *The Way Things Were.*

Chapter 6

First Visit To The Walker Farm

School was over. I had managed to survive the first grade, and Mrs. Mason, the first grade teacher, had said to my mother that I was a good student…very inquisitive. I asked Mother what inquisitive meant; she said that I was very active and "nosey", but in a nice way. I later learned that to be inquisitive was good, but also that I could get into a whole lot of trouble by being too inquisitive, especially out in the country on a farm.

"Tomorrow, we are going to Grandpa's Farm," my older brother, Billy said. He had overheard Mother and Dad talking about driving up to Grandpa's farm in Millen, Georgia when school was out for the summer.

Well, it looked like that day had finally arrived.

Billy and I had packed our clothes and toys. I also went around the neighborhood trading my old comic books for the new editions of Bugs Bunny, Captain Marvel, Superman, The Lone Ranger, Popeye, Donald Duck and Dick Tracy, to name a few. I had gotten the newest and best

30

books I could get with the front covers still on and without missing pages.

I was ready to go and looked forward to seeing real live cows, horses and hogs. Also I had heard that Grandpa had lots of watermelons and I loved watermelons. I wasn't allowed to eat any watermelons near bedtime because sometimes I was just too lazy at night to get up and go to the bathroom and would wet the bed at night. The car was hot and the sun was in my face. That's what woke me up from my sleep.

I could hear Daddy whistling as we zoomed down highway #301 at sixty-five miles per hour in his 1941 white Plymouth. "Are we there yet, Daddy," I asked.

"No, not yet", Daddy replied. "Hey, Bee, we gonna have to stop soon and feed the children. Bee, are you awake, Bee?"

Mother said, "I hear you, Charlie." She yawned and stretched her arms. She looked down at Elaine, my baby sister, who had fallen asleep just a soon as we started driving. "Look for a nice shady spot with some bushes and trees, so we can go to the bathroom. I got to go and I know these children got to go."

This was in 1945 when colored folks traveling by car up and down the highways in southern states were accustomed to using trees, bushes and ditches and other forms of nature as toilets. No colored person would dare travel without toilet paper and picnic baskets filled with water, sodas and food.

Yea, I was about to bust. I learned later, as I got older, that I had a "weak bladder", and I had many spankings and very embarrassing moments in my life before I learned how to control my urination.

We ate some of the sandwiches Mother had prepared for the trip, peanut butter with jelly, bologna and cheese with sandwich spread or mayonaise. Mother also had fried chicken and biscuits with strawberry jam and a bottle of syrup.

Daddy always ate biscuits and syrup at every meal; no matter what the main menu, Daddy always ate syrup and biscuits. Mother had learned about Daddy's habit from his mother, Grandma Louise Walker, who taught Mother how to cook all of Daddy's favorite foods before she and Dad "jumped the broom"…married.

This trip was especially memorable, not only because it was my first time going to the Farm (that is as a big boy of seven years old), but it was also the first time I learned about "Jim Crow" and "segregation".

Sometime later in the day, I remember Daddy saying. "We are almost out of gas, guess I'll pull over at the next gas station." I remember telling Daddy, I had to pee. "Me, too", said Elaine, who had crawled over the front seat and was sitting between Billy and me. "You smell like you just done number two."

"That wasn't me." Elaine said. And of course, we continued to make fun of her until Daddy stopped the car and I heard him say. "Fill her up" to the white boy who came up to the car from the garage. He looked much older than Billy and I, but I could tell he was still a boy. He didn't have any hair on his face and he had freckles, long red hair and brown teeth from chewing tobacco. He started putting gas in the car and said, "Hey, Boy, where ya'll comin' frum?"

I started to answer, thinking he was talking to me or Billy, but when I looked at him he was looking straight at Daddy, and asked the same question again. I thought he sure is dumb to be calling a grown man a boy. Daddy ignored him and said, "The bathroom for colored is around back, I 'spect?"

The white boy shook his head. "Naw, we ain't got no piss house fer niggers, yaw'l got to use the woods out back"!

Daddy said "don't you put another drop of gas in my car!" He gave the boy $1.25 for five gallons of gas. I looked at Daddy's face and saw the two rows of skin wrinkle up between his eyebrows. (That's the sign that he is angry)

Bill & I had figured the moods of Daddy by certain facial expressions and sounds he made years earlier. When the skin was smooth between Daddy's eyes he was in a good mood; when he was whistling he was in a happy, joyful mood. So we tried to always keep the skin smooth or we would do our best to keep Daddy whistling.

Daddy said, "I don't spend my money nowhere that ain't got bath rooms for us and I don't like going to the back door either. That's why your Mother fixed us food to eat, so we don't ever have to go to no white man's back door." Yes sir! Daddy was mad.

That was my introduction to Jim Crow; and Daddy's words rang loud and clear in my ears all my life. As an adult, my motto is, "I am a man and I go through the front door or I don't go in at all."

It wasn't too long before we got off the main highway, # 301, and got on a yellow/red dust road. Daddy slowed down but it still felt as if we were riding on railroad ties there were so many bumps. As we looked out the window we could see dust flying out behind us. It was fun for us kids as we went up one hill and down another like a roller coaster.

We could see fields of tall, green, flowing plants that we later called "corn stalks". Then we saw fields that looked white as snow from a distance, but as we got closer we could see the little white bolls attached to the stems, which was "cotton".

We saw horses and mules in corrals, running around tossing their head as we flew past the many farms. There were tin top houses and log barns with open windows and haylofts.

As we passed each farm, we saw little colored boys and girls our ages waving at us. There were also older children and adults in the cotton fields. We could see them bending down between the rows of cotton plants with long Crocker sacks across their shoulders. (Later Billy and I learned how to pick as much as fifty pounds of cotton per day!)

We saw colored women "drawing water" from outdoor wells and older ladies in rocking chairs on front porches that were build around the houses. The houses were built two to three feet off the ground.

Everybody seemed glad to see us as we went speeding by. They were all waving and grinning, with white teeth gleaming and they were yelling "hello, hello". But, Daddy was not slowing down. On and On we rode. The sun was doing down in the west, but it was still hot and dusty. However, for some reason I was too excited to be hot. The entire countryside was amazing to me. I was used to seeing flat land with orange groves, but this land had hills and red, red clay and different kinds of trees.

We saw fields of trees with yellow pears, reddish peaches, and dark blue plums. Soon we came around a sharp curve and Daddy slowed down. "Well, here it is, boys. Look Chicken, (Elaine) there's my old home place. That's the Walker Farm!"

Daddy started blowing the horn as we drove up this long circular driveway with pecan trees on each side. He stopped the car at a wooden gate, which opened into a large yard with a long red brick walkway leading up to wooden steps. Down those steps came two people that I would learn to love and respect...Grandma Susie (who was Grandpa's third wife) and Grandpa Alfred. He was about seventy years old then, but had the strength and ability of a thirty-year old man.

Little did I know about the farm life, about fruits, about plants, animals and people. Little did I know about anything! But I would learn. Oh, yes, I would learn so much on the farm; and this was my first summer of a time and place that now is only a memory. I cherish those days

Robert J. Walker (Bobby)

and years of so long ago because that was the beginning of
The Way The Way Things Were.

Chapter 7

Blackie

It's often said that, "A man's best friend is a dog". That may be so. As children growing up in Sebring, Florida we Walkers had our share of dogs as pets.

Both of my parents were animal and nature lovers and taught us at a very early age that "God, The Creator, gave mankind dominion over the earth and the animals, and that we were to help preserve and care for them.

But it wasn't a dog that made the greatest impression on me as a child. It was a black female cat that Mother had gotten from some white folks that she ironed clothes for once per week.

Let me see, it must have been around 1947-48 when I was in the fourth grade. I came home from school one day and while we were eating supper Mother said, "Charlie, Mrs. Piety's cat had a litter of kittens and she gave me one. You think we could let the kids keep her?"

My Mother knew how to get my Dad to do what she wanted, she had waited until he had finished his main meal and now, was eating what was his desert. (sopping syrup with hot biscuits) If I had neglected to mention it before, sopping syrup with hot biscuits was something Dad did after each meal and we children also develop the taste for syrup and biscuits. But, we were not allowed to have this "treat" until we had cleaned our plates of the main meal. By dangling this sweet treat over my head Mother managed to get me to eat spinach, liver, carrots, beets, and oatmeal.

"Well, what do you think, Charlie?'

Dad drank from his cup, cleared his throat and said: "Bee, "it's ok for the kids to keep that cat, but it's clear they the ones that gonna care for it, that means feeding and cleaning up after that cat done messed up."

"Is that clear?"

"Yes sir! Yes, sir, thank you Dad. Thank you, Mom." We gladly agreed.

Elaine said, "We gonna call her Blackie cause she is sooo black.

Well, that settled the matter, we had ourselves a cat called "Blackie, and soon she was responding to that name. When one of us would say, "Here Blackie, kitty, kitty" she would come running up from where ever she was…under the house, out in the field, down the street, up a tree, it didn't matter. All we (even Dad or Mother)had to do was yell, "Here Blackie, kitty, kitty"!

Weeks passed. Months passed and soon Blackie was a grown up adult cat. Pretty soon at night I could hear the male cats, pawing, screaming and mating with Blackie, and…it wasn't long before Blackie gave birth to a litter of kittens.

One morning at breakfast Daddy said, "Billy, Bobby, y'all got to git rid of those kittens. We got enough mouths to feed without them. So by weekend they got to go. Y'all hear me?"

There wasn't any need to say anything more on the subject, Daddy had spoken. Therefore, all week long Billy and I were telling our friends to come over to our house and pick out a kitten. They were very cute little kittens and four out of the nine were buck-tailed, which meant that one of those Tom Cats we heard fighting in the night to mate with Blackie was a Florida Bob Cat with a short tail. Of course,

Dad and Mother explained all the sexability and mating process to us.

Elaine fell in love with one of the Buck-tailed kittens she called "Buck". "Daddy, can I keep Buck? He won't be no trouble, he can eat my milk. Please Daddy, I want to keep him."

Needless to say, Elaine was Daddy's little girl. He called her "Chicken" and all she had to do was roll those big beautiful black eyes up at him and give him her pretty smile with a hug and he was putty...

"O.K., O. K., but that's it. No more cats, kittens, dogs, chickens, rabbits! Y'all hear me? We got enough animals around this house."

We saw the wrinkle in his forehead and we knew that he was serious. We finally managed to give away all the kittens and all was well and quiet for several weeks or maybe a couple of months.

But it wasn't long before we heard those familiar cat sounds at night again and sure enough some time later we noticed Blackie outback near the wash house with a baby

42

kitten in her mouth. "Billy, where do you think she is going with that baby kitten?"

"I don't know," he said, "Let's follow her." We followed Blackie and watched her make the trip from the wash house to a corner underneath the front porch. She made that trip eight times as she moved a litter from the wash house to the corner spot under the front porch.

One Friday evening at supper, Daddy said, "I've had enough, Bee. That female cat got to go. All she gonna do is keep having kittens and we can't keep them." (Back then in the forties most colored people couldn't afford to doctor up pets to stop them from breeding)

Elaine cried, and cried, even my big brother Billy had a tear in his eye as we pleaded with Daddy. I said, "Me and Billy will chase the Tom cats away from her. Please Daddy don't take her away."

Daddy said, "You got one cat, Buck, one dog Patsy. That's enough extra mouths to feed, not counting all dem chickens and rabbits out back."

The next morning (Saturday) we saw Daddy with a large crocker sack. He got in the truck and told Mother he was going to the city dump, which was about six miles outside of the city limits.

"I'm gonna take that cat and all her brood to the city dump. They can find shelter and plenty food out there to eat."

We children cried and for several days we missed Blackie, but as the weeks went by, we played with Buck and our dog Patsy. Then one afternoon Elaine called me. "Bobby, come here". I was on the side of the house playing Cowboy and Indian with my friend, Connie.

I said, "Elaine, whatcha want?" She said, "Come here, look at this cat, I think it's Blackie."

I ran around to the back yard. Sure nuff, there was this Black cat by the wash shed. Elaine got on her knees and called, "Here Blackie," and Blackie cam trotting up to her...

When Dad got home that evening he wasn't pleased at all, and we heard him talking to Mother. "That cat came back here after three weeks and six miles. Next time I'll have to take her further away."

It was after Dad had gone away on one of his business trips, that we missed Blackie and realized that she was gone. Daddy had taken Blackie away again. We missed her all over again, but we didn't dare say anything, because we knew that the matter was settled. Dad had done what he thought was best for the family.

I was in the fourth grade when Blackie was taken away. Months passed and months turned into years. And soon we all forgot about Blackie.

"Patsy and Buck were our house pets and we had pigeons that roosted in the front porch ceiling. We had chickens out back, so we had plenty enough pets around the house and Blackie was never mentioned especially in Daddy's presence.

One cold Saturday morning in 1950 Mother reminded me, "Bobby, come on, now get out of that bed and get that fire started under that kettle, I got a whole lot of sheets to wash today."

Dad was already up and in the bathroom. As soon as he came out I went in. I could hear Billy and Elaine in the kitchen talking to Mother. She was opening the back door saying, "The sun is shinning so bright this is gonna be a good wash day". Then suddenly "My gosh, will you look at this poor skinny cat out her on the back steps."

Elaine said, "He's so dirty, looks like oil on his fur."

Billy said, "His ribs are showing and his ear is bleeding, he must have been in a fight."

I came out of the bathroom and started to the back porch to see the cat when Mother said, "Bobby bring a little milk and a dish and some of that cornbread from the ice box."

Mother took the dish and crumbled the cornbread in the milk and as she went down the steps. The cat said, "Meow, Meow". And Mother looked closely and screamed, "Oh, my Lord, I believe, I think this is Blackie." She got down on her knees and held out the dish and called: "Here Blackie, here, kitty, kitty, Blackie come here."

I was standing at the back screen door and I watched that skinny, dirty, ugly wounded cat struggle up those steps, I watched and cried with joy as she slowly rubbed her head under Mother's out stretched hand…

Mother said to me with tears running down her face, "Bobby, you go tell your Daddy that Blackie done come home.!"

Later that evening when we all sat down for supper and Dad blessed the food, he gave a little extra thanks with his eyes watering up. "Lord, we sure nuff thank you for this food and all your blessing…and Lord we thank you for this cat we call "Blackie". It's been more than two years and she has traveled unknown miles through woods, through cities, and highway traffic. She suffered through cold winter nights and hot summers days and you know what else, to git back here to this house…well, Lord this is sure nuff her home now…and I'll never take her away again. Amen."

Note:

Dad spoke of Blackie today (December 13, 2001). He told me that it was the most amazing thing he could think of, that he has seen a lot in over 90 years of living. You see, He took Blackie over near Tampa, Florida that last time he took her away. (70 or 80 miles)

Blackie lived to a ripe old age (14 years) and she was Daddy's special pet and the queen of the Walker's household. We buried her out back near the wash shed in 1962, the year I graduated from college. And this is another chapter in *The Way Things Were*.

Chapter 8

Musical Raindrops

"Billy, Bobby, Elaine! Come on in this house. It's getting ready to rain!"

Oh, no, not today! Why does it always have to rain on Saturday? Brother Billy and I had just almost finished repairing our Box Car, which Billy and I made ourselves. In fact, all of the Colored kids (boys and girls) knew how to make a Box Car in those days. (1945-55)

. . . .

To make a Box Car, first get a fruit box from around the fruit packing houses or sometimes you could find an old one left behind in an orange grove. These crate boxes were made of wood about three feet long with a section in the middle. We would take the section out, so it was large enough to sit or kneel down in the box.

We used a 2' x 4' board six-feet long as the main axle. Also two 2' x 4" two-feet long were used to connect the

49

wheels, which were gotten from old baby carriages. Rope was tied to the front axle and used to steer or guide the Box Car by pulling the rope to the right or left. Your feet dragging in the ground served as brakes.

....

Why couldn't it rain tomorrow when we were in church or better still wait until Monday morning when we were in school in Miss Daniel's fifth grade class! She usually kept us singing except on days when it was raining then she made us put our heads on the desk and be very quiet. You can even go to sleep, which is what most of us children did.

You see, Miss Daniels was a Christian and she wouldn't allow us to talk when it was raining with thunder and lightening. She said, "God was talking and watering His garden." She often would say, "God is in control and you do not tell Him when to water His garden."

Mother called again, "You children hear me? Hurry in, it is starting to rain." As soon as we get on the front porch, we could look down the clay roads (Zion and Harris Streets) and see the rain drops. As they hit the dry red clay a puff of sand would splatter, one drop, two drops, then three drops, then many drops falling, falling. Soon it was like a sheet or wall of raindrops, huge raindrops. You could hear the rain splattering on the ground and on the tin top roof of our house and then a cool wind beginning to blow.

Wind coming up from the southwest "means a thunder storm". "Alright, now, get into this house! Hurry up! Close all the windows. This is going to be a big one. Just might bring your dad home early. He sure can't pick any fruit in this rain." Mother said that Daddy worked so often on so many jobs that she was extremely happy when he came home early due to rain. I didn't pay much attention to what mother was saying. But later, when I got older I remembered that part about "Sure can't pick fruit in this rain!"

For a moment or two I stood at the window and looked at the water making little red rivers in the dirt road, water puddles forming little lakes in the front lawns. I saw blue jays and mocking birds making last minute flights from one china berry tree to another and then over to our large Georgia pecan tree and several palm trees. The little sparrows were already hidden way back up in the branches of the two Australian Pines, which were in our front yard.

Stray dogs were running to get under the cars that were parked along the street or in someone's yard. As I pressed my face against the window pane my imaginative mind turned the pecan tree leaves into ships or boats. They sailed down the little rivers in the road, faster and faster they came. Some times the raindrops would sink the ships and then it would pop up further down the road.

"Boom! Cracked! Boom! The lightening flashed and the thunder roared! I jumped away from the window just as Elaine screamed and Mother said, "Bobby get in here and sit with us or go to bed."

I chose to join Billy in the bed, where he was already sleeping. A few years earlier I would have elected to go sit near Mother and have her hold me and hum a sweet song. Mother was a credited opera singer. Since I was older then, lightening and thunder didn't frighten me. But I wished Billy would wake up, not that I was scared. But I got up to make sure our bedroom door was open so Mother can hear us and peep in the door and I went to pull down the window shades…we didn't have venetian blinds then in the fifties.

I mean, I don't mind listening to God talk, but I don't have to look at His words. (Lightening) So back in the bed and under the covers I go. I put the pillow over my head and I closed my eyes and, it rained and rained. Soon the lightening stopped and a steady rain started, not really hard, but with a light beat and rhythm.

I removed the pillow from over my head and listened. Rain drops falling on the tin top roof…drip, drop…drip, drip, drop…like music, a high pitch, a low pitch…a bass pitch, a tenor pitch…soprano and alto pitch. It sounded like a band playing! Music on a tin top roof!

Mother had taught us and also Miss Daniels had told us that "When it is raining, God is watering His garden. When it is thundering and lightening God is talking".

But I discovered something else that Saturday afternoon so long ago, when it was raining; God can also play music! I heard Him playing a melody that day when the rain fell on a tin top roof…drip, drop…drip, drip, drop…musical notes.

Robert J. Walker (Bobby)

And that's the way things were long, long ago on a rainy afternoon.

Chapter 9

Hi Yo Silver

This past Thanksgiving, November 2000, I looked at my grand children playing with all the many computer games and other video games that can be connected to the television. Then there are the hundred or so board games that can be purchased at toy stores like Radio Shack, Walmart, K-Mart, Eckerds and Walgreen Drug Stores. Yet just a few days ago I heard a neighbor's ten-year-old boy tell his dad that he was bored with nothing to do.

My mind went back to the "Good Old Days" when I was around ten years old in the fourth grade. I was asthmatic and rather obese, since I wasn't allowed to do much running or exercising. I changed all of that when I got older. I ate a lot and read all of the comic books that I could get my hands on. Telling my parents I was bored never came to my mind.

My brother, sister and I learned how to create and make up things to do to entertain ourselves. Just to mention a few…cowboys and Indians was a favorite past time game.

We cut bamboo reeds, bent the top of the reed, tied a rope on one end and ran around with the long reed between our legs. The reeds acted as our horses. Any piece of wood could be whittled into the shape or a gun.

On special occasions, sometimes Dad would purchase cap guns or water pistols for us for birthdays or Christmas; but usually the "store bought" pistols wouldn't last but a month or two and then we had to make our own guns again.

Another game we made up was car racing, but we didn't use a store bought toy car, instead we used real car tires. Yes, I would get an old tire and push it with my hands. Of course, I used my mind and voice "brrrr…varoomming…sputter and reeeunnnee" as I ran down the road pushing the tire or rolling the tire as fast as I could run. This game was tiring and with asthma I didn't run too fast or too far; but it was fun, especially when all the neighborhood kids would get together and have "tire races".

Later on Dad taught us how to build carts. (I will discuss this in a later chapter.) Building carts requires carpenter skills and other abilities. We also spent a lot of time climbing trees…oak trees, china berry trees, guava trees, blueberry trees, Japanese or China plum trees, coconut trees and most of all orange, grapefruit and tangerine trees. I could climb real good and sometimes I climbed almost to the very top and hide from my brother and sister.

My main hobby was listening to the radio and that is what I was doing as this story unfolds…listening to a radio show called "The Lone Ranger".

"Billy, Bobby, it's time to git up!" That was my dad calling me and my brother. He usually calls us only once as he passes our bedroom on his way to the bathroom. He usually takes about 20 to 25 minutes to do what all gown men do in the early morning hours in the bathroom.

"Billy, you git up and go see if you caught any fish in your trap." That's my ma. She's getting ready to cook breakfast and since this is a Saturday and we don't have school, we have some extra time before breakfast is ready.

Billy is out of bed, has his clothes on and running out the back door, before I finally roll out of bed. It's a little cold and I start sneezing as soon as my feet touch the cold floor. "Bobby, put your house shoes on before you catch a cold." Mother said, "and it's your turn to put some wood on the fireplace." "Yes, Mam" I said to her and started getting dressed for the day.

I soon had a big fire going in the fireplace and the house started warming up. I could hear Billy cleaning the fish. (Bass, bluegill, catfish) He had gotten from the fish traps we set. Dad had taught us how to set fish lines and fish traps in Dinner Lake. It wasn't long before we all sat down to a Saturday morning breakfast of fish, grits, biscuits, hush puppies, eggs, gravy and syrup. Daddy always had biscuits and syrup regardless if we were eating breakfast, dinner or supper.

"Billy, you and Bobby got the yard to do today, and I don't want no boys over here playing till all your work is done; and Bobby you stay away from that radio, hear me, boy?

"Yes, sir Dad. I'm gonna do all my work first, O.K.?"

"Charlie, I'm going to do a half day at Mr. Piety's and then I'll be home. Elaine, you clean up your room and pick up a few things around the house. Make it real nice and clean for me, Sweetie."

"O.K., Mother, I'll do a good job"'. That's my sister, Elaine, and yes, she would do a good job. In fact, it usually is an excellent job. She loves to outdo Billy and me and make us look bad. But then I didn't care. Who wanted to clean house...that's a sissy job anyway. A man's job was outside in the yard or working on cars...things like that...things that got your hands dirty and sweat running down your arms and face.

A man's work meant wiping sweat from your forehead with a red bandana, drinking water from the water hose and then running some water over your head to cool off. That's man work, yeah!

Oh well, Mother and Dad both left for work and pretty soon we three Walker children were busy with our Saturday morning chores. The sun was shining bright and that helped to keep me warm because it was still chilly and even though I was cutting the hedges, moving my arms and hands it was still kinda cold...about 40-45 degrees. Back in the 1940's the weather was much colder during the winter months.

"Billy, you wanna take a break?"

"Naw, Bobby. Let's do the whole yard all at once then we can go inside".

I said, "Good idea! Maybe we can finish in time for 'The Long Ranger' show. We continued working, mowing the lawn, cutting the hedges, raking the leaves and cleaning out around the flower beds and walkways.

At 11:50 a.m. we were done; we put away the tools, washed our hands, changed our clothes and were stretched out in the front of our living room RCA radio. It was a large standup model with an open shelf in the lower center portion. This model was very popular in 1947-48 but very few colored folks could afford one. Dad and Mother were about the first colored people to own a stand-up RCA radio in Sebring, Florida.

"Hi Yo Silver. It's the Lone Ranger and his friend Tonto." The music could be heard all over the house, even my sister, Elaine, came and sat down to listen. We were so engrossed in the story we didn't hear Daddy's truck drive up out front. Beep, Beep.

"Billy, you and Bobby come out here", Dad called us. When we got to the door, we could see his face; the lines between his eyes were smooth, which meant he was in a good mood. We went outside and Dad said, "I want you two boys to take this chicken feed around the back. Give a little to the chickens and then put this bag in the wash shed for safe keeping. Ya'll hear me? And git the 'wheelbarrel' so you don't spill none".

"Yes, Sir, Daddy". We both told Dad and he got into the truck and drove off. It was a real simple chore, and all we had to do was to go around to the back yard, get the wheelbarrel, place the 100 pound bag of chicken feed on the wheelbarrow…push the wheelbarrel slowly around to the back yard. Take the chicken feed off the wheelbarrel, open it up, take two or three scoops of chicken feed and feed the chickens; take the rest of the chicken feed and pull, shove, pull the bag into the wash shed, close the door, go back to the living room and continue listening to the Lone Ranger radio show.

Now, what I just described above might have taken no more than six to ten minutes with Billy and I working together…but for some reason we didn't see it that way. The easy way would be to pick up the bag and carry it in a hurry to the back yard. (After all, we don't want to miss too much of the Long Ranger show) Then we proceeded to pick up the 100-pound bag of chicken feed and yes, we were even trying to run with it. Billy had one end and I had the other end. And yes, you guessed it. We got to the corner of the house where the walkway ends and the grass and sand begin.

I stumbled and my brother, Billy, fell down and the chicken feed bag burst open...corn mash went flying everywhere all over the yard, grass, sidewalk, sand, and hedges.

Now, once again the smartest thing to do would be to take our time and pick up, rake up, sweep up, brush up, even vacuum up or eat up as much of that chicken feed as we could. But, being not too bright or smart and being in a hurry to get back to "Hi YO Silver" we decided to do the fastest thing. "Cover up the spilled chicken feed". Yeah, that was really bright. It almost worked.

I say, "almost" because it was sometime later in the evening before Dad came home. In fact, Mother had come home and dinner was being prepared and we (Billy, Elaine and I) had been listening to "The Shadow Knows", another favorite radio program.

We could hear Daddy's whistling, which meant he was in a very good mood. We could hear his whistle as he came into the yard. The whistling continued as he walked on the sidewalk and then, he came to the corner of the house. The whistling stopped. We strained our ears to hear some more whistling, but we could hear nothing...only silence...more silence. I looked at Billy. Billy looked at me and the voice that we feared to hear came booming around the house through the back door, through the front door, through the side door, through the open windows and even down the chimney.

"Billy, Bobby! Git out here and I mean quick!" The voice said it all. He had found evidence of our crime. He had discovered the covered up chicken feed. I mean it was almost dark outside, how could he see those little pieces of yellow corn? And another thing, he was supposed to be happy whistling with his head looking up. He wasn't supposed to be looking down on the ground. But, "our goose was cooked!" He had the evidence in his hand and was searching the ground for more corn.

"You boy's didn't do like I told you! You wasted my chicken feed all over the yard. You both were in such a hurry you didn't use the wheelbarrow like I told you, did you?"

"Go git a flash light and some paper bags. Ya'll come git every grain of this corn off this ground. I mean in the grass, hedges, sand, where ever...even if it takes you all night!"

Well, that incident took place over fifty years ago and I haven't forgotten it to this day. We, Billy and I, stayed up most of the night picking up corn seed, grain, etc. that we spilled and then tried to cover up and hide.

I learned a lot from that incident: (1) Be obedient. If only we had obeyed Dad and taken our time and used the wheelbarrow. (2) After spilling the chicken feed, we should have cleaned up thoroughly and gotten all of the grain up instead of covering it up. (3) "Haste sometimes makes wastes" But you know what? I still miss hearing that old familiar voice and music of the radio. "Hi YO Silver,

Away" and that was the Way Things Were" so long ago in 1947-48 in a small southern city called Sebring, Florida.

Chapter 10

The Church Day in Millen, Georgia

My mind wandered back to the good old days of summer when Billy, and I would spend our vacation with Grandpa Walker and Grandma Susie in Millen, Georgia in the summer of 1950.

"Bobby, you hurry up taking your bath; I gotta take me one." That's Billy for you, waiting to the last moment then "he get in a hurry and expect everybody to jump 'cause he say so...or he could have taken his bath on Saturday night; but then neither one of us took our baths like Grandpa had suggested. Instead, we selected to take an early morning bath before going to church."

Naturally, I took my time bathing, then carrying out the dirty water, dumping it in the back yard. I stood there a while watching the water run down hill until it joined another little stream which was caused by the water coming from the sides of the well. It's been said that "Grandpa Walker's well had the sweetest water in all of Macon

County and that the spring that filled the well never ran dry, regardless of the length of the drought.

Billy came outside, got the tub and filled it with well water to take his bath and I went inside to get dressed for church. Sunday morning church started at 11 a.m. By then I had learned that out here in the country, folks stayed at the church all day long. It was fun…girls, singing, shouting, eating, testifying, singing, sleeping, more fun, more girls. Oh yes, and some preaching.

Around 8:30 a.m. Grandma Susie called us to breakfast of ham, eggs, grits, flour bread, syrup, along with milk and coffee for Grandpa and Grandma. Meals at Grandpa's house were always a very exciting and interesting event, because Grandpa ate everything with a knife. Now as strange as that may seem, it's true. We, his grandchildren, talked about that even today at this years's 2000 Walker's reunion how Grandpa Alfred Walker would mix his eggs and grits together, then eat with his knife.

Then Grandma Susie would bring him biscuits and syrup. He would "sop" the syrup with the biscuits. Another thing that Grandpa would do that would have us kids laughing at the table, Grandpa would close his eyes and chew his food. Sometimes it looked as though he was sleeping, but then he would say, "You boys done finish eating? Then take your plates to the kitchen" It was fun to see him eat peas, corn or beans with that knife; but he could do it and not a single pea or bean would fall off that knife on the way to his mouth.

After breakfast, we could hear Grandpa getting the mules ready to "hook up" to the "Sunday-go-meeting-wagon."…"git back mule, whoa Red, hold still dere, now boy, back - back, boy, dat's right, whoa dere."

I could listen to Grandpa all day talking to them mules like they could understand every thing he said…maybe they could, cause they usually obeyed him.

At 9 a.m. we started to church, about five miles away, Brimson Rock Baptist Church. "Git up dere, Red". Grandpa and Grandma sat up front on the riding bench. Billy and I sat on the back at the very end of the wagon so our feet slightly touched the ground…the wagon wheels kicking up dust and Big Red walking at an easy gait. I think Grandpa had driven this route to church so many times he knew that at a five miles per hour pace, we would get to church just about on time for 11 a.m. service.

Grandma Susie started humming a tune, and soon she was singing out loud, "gonna lay down my burden, down by the river side, down by the river side". Pretty soon all of us were singing, clapping our hands and having a good time.

As we came to a cross road, we could see Mr. & Mrs. Jenkins' wagon with their two children, Evelyn and Junior riding on the back. Another wagon was coming down the road with a bunch of kids on the back. This was also a fun time because, before long there would be a caravan of buggies, wagons, riders on horse back or mules and maybe a few old model T Fords all heading in the same direction...To Brimson Rock Baptist Church.

As I look back to the years 1948-1955, I remember Sunday's being a very special day...people on the farms back during those days came to church to give God thanks, and to praise Him for good crops, good health and very little sickness. The people also came to fellowship with each other. They used this meeting and coming together as a social gathering also.

When morning church was over around 1 p.m., the ladies would spread blankets and bring out the picnic baskets. I can smell the food even to this day…fired chicken, collard greens, biscuits, cornbread, corn cobs, potato salad, sausage, pig feet, beans, rice, cakes, pies, sweet bread, bread pudding, lemonade, iced tea, sweet water and just plain cool well water.

This eating time was the very best for us children. We were allowed to go to any body's table or blanket. We could eat as much as we wanted just as long as we remembered our manners. Say "thank you," "please", "excuse me", "I'm sorry", "Hello and goodbye".

We knew to wash our hands before and after eating and not to talk while our mouths were full of food. Most of all, we knew not to put on our plate more than we could eat. Grandpa called that "Your eyes are bigger than your stomach".

After eating, the children would find games to play or go running or walking in the near by corn or cotton fields or down the roadside. The grownups would sit under oak or pine trees or just stretch out on a blanket and take a little nap. Some of the older women would spend this time gossiping and the older men sometimes talked about fishing or crops or how the farm animals were breeding.

Evening Sunday service would soon start again around 5.p.m. and last until 8 p.m. The time at church varied depending on time of year. Summer days were much longer.

Going back home at night was a little scary when Billy and I were young. It was dark at night and riding on that old buckboard wagon was slow and creepy. Every night sound and every dark shadow brought fear to our little child minds.

But as we got older and our new interested in girls started to materialize the after evening church rides were the best of times. But, that's another story in *The Way Things Were.*

Chapter 11

A Colored Band In The Christmas Parade

I remember Mrs. Morgan, the white music teacher, who taught us colored children piano and singing at E. O. Douglas School one to twelve grades in Sebring, Florida.

One day Mrs. Morgan asked, "How many of you would like to learn to play other instruments besides the piano, like the trumpet, clarinet, or saxophone?"

Just about all of us eighth graders held our hands up that day, and it was only a few weeks when Mr. Samuel Nixon (principal of E. O. Douglas School) called an assembly meeting for junior and senior high school students in the cafeteria.

"Boys and girls, I am pleased to introduce Mr. Heilm who owns a music store downtown off the Circle. He will be teaching you to play the different instruments that are in a band, because that is what we are going to have here at E. O. Douglas…a school band!"

I remember clearly the excitement, the yelling, the clapping of hands and everybody asking, "How can I sign up?" "When are we going to start?" "Where are the instruments?" "Who is going to pay for the instruments?"

Mr. Nixon's next statement was, "Any person interested in getting an instrument on time payments, fill out these papers that I am passing out and take them home to your parents to read and sign. You will then be contacted by Mr. Heilm and your parents can arrange a payment plan.

Well, that's the way I remember the E. O. Douglas marching band getting started.

Many colored parents went into debt for the next two to three years signing up for trumpets - $200.00, saxophones - $250.00, clarinets - $100.00, trombones - $250.00, drums - $100.00, flutes - $95.00, French horns - $275.00 and other instruments that we had never heard of...tubas and zellophones. Many youths had their parents spend hard earned money for an instrument that they would try to play for a few weeks and then stop; but then the parents had to continue paying for the instrument or let another parent, who had a child begging to play in the band, continue to make the payments.

Several months later Mr. Nixon called another assembly and introduced the first and only band director at E. O. Douglas High School at that time. Mr. Walter Beard, who was a recent graduate from Bethune Cookman College and was so amazing to us Negro children. We had never seen anyone up close or in real life who could play the trumpet, clarinet, saxophone, trombone, and beat a drum too. I later learned that Mr. Beard and could master every instrument that we had in the band.

I begged my parents for a saxophone, but Daddy decided that $200.00 was too much to waste on a "toy" that I would get tired of in a few months. Therefore, I got a clarinet for $50.00. (the brass-silver type, but I later purchased a black wood clarinet.) I immediately liked the clarinet. It was easy to carry and the mouthpiece was perfect for my lips and teeth. Mr. Beard later told me that the shape of my mouth and protruding teeth made it easier for me to play reed instruments. (sax's, clarinets, etc.)

Most of my childhood friends were in the band: Connie Shorte - trumpet, Spenser Burgess - clarinet, Robert Burgess – snare drum, Nancy Mckenney – clarinet, Elaine Walker– zellophone, Allonzo Richards – saxophone, Ron Brown – trumpet, Donald Watson - snare drum, Alfred Cooper – clarinet, Joe Jackson – trombone, Bernie Shoates – French horn.

We boys played in the band during the eighth grade and the first semester of the ninth grade we later joined the football and basketball teams, which limited us to playing only in the concert band and not the marching band.

This arrangement was very difficult for Mr. Beard because during football season most of all his clarinet, drum and trumpet male players were playing football. But it was the first year in the marching band that I recall so clearly, and vividly. I can still hear the first song that we learned to play and march to…"Washington Post".

"We are going to learn this piece to play", said Mr. Beard, "You will learn it so well that you will be humming it when you go to bed, whistling it when you awaken in the morning. We will learn this tune so well that you will never forget it as long as you live! So practice, practice, practice and more practice. Bobby Walker, you and Alfred Cooper and Spencer Burgess will play first clarinet. Connie Shorte, you and Freddie Lorket will be first trumpet and so on…

Mr. Beard gave us all our positions in the band according to our playing ability…and boy did we practice! I mean you could hear instruments all over Washington Heights in the afternoon after school. It seems like every youth who was in the band would get out on their front or back porch after school and practice Washington Post.

If I forgot to practice after getting home from school and completing my chores, I would hear Alfred blowing his clarinet and that would remind me to practice.

While growing up in Sebring, Florida I was exposed to Jim Crow…segregated facilities, restrooms, water fountains, drug store soda fountains, circle park, movie theater and I had many degrading, humiliating experiences as a child. But I learned how to be smart as a fox, especially when I was around other cultures how to observe, how to listen, but act dumb and be slow to speak and only when it was appropriate and necessary. When talking to white folks

I learned how to give short respectful answers. "Yes sir, no sir" and don't volunteer any information. How to look the white person directly in his or her eyes and not show any emotion. These were just a few of the survival skills I learned as a child. But getting back to the band...

Mr. Beard came to the band practice that November day in 1952 and announced "We re going to march in the downtown Sebring Christmas Parade. Now that doesn't mean much to anyone reading this story at the present period in time. But back then in 1952-1953 it was a very big thing. In fact, history was being made. Can you imagine a "Colored band in the Christmas Parade"...the very first time anything like that had ever been done in Sebring.

Well needless to say, it was the talk of the town, especially in colored town (Washington Heights). People were excited and full of anticipation. What uniforms were we going to wear? Can we march good enough? Can we keep up? How will the white folks treat us? What will we play?

The first three questions were answered within the next two or three weeks, but the last question was answered almost immediately. Every band member knew that we were going to march to Washington Post! The fourth question would have to wait until parade day.

The day of the parade finally arrived and we were all down behind the old white Sebring High School getting in position to march up Center Street Toward the Circle and then down North Ridgewood Drive passing Gilbert's Drug Store, the Five and Ten Cent Store, the old Salvation Army Building, Bob's Men's Wear, Wilson's Shoe Store, the Nancessowee and other shops which were on the main drag or main street.

The parade finally started and we (the colored band)…yes, you guessed it…were placed at the very end of the parade and finally the answer to 4th question.

I remember so well as we marched around the Circle, we were stepping so high in our home-made uniforms…black pants, white shirt, black tie, black shoes, black socks and no hats. All forty of us were dressed exactly alike with no different colored shoes or socks, but all black. Many parents sacrificed to purchase material and make or have their outfits made.

We marched with our feet and heads held high and our instruments swinging from side to side like Florida A. & M. marching band. Every now and then, Clarence Barnes, the head drum major would blow his whistle twice "tweep, tweep" and turn to face the band while marching backwards a few steps. He would start us on "Washington Post."

Mr. Beard also wore black pants, white shirt and black coat as he marched by our side. Over and over we played Washington Post; we must have played it at least seven times that day.

As we made the final turn onto Ridgewood and heading North traveling toward Pine Street, (we were now on "Main Street" in Sebring, Florida) I thought of all the practice sessions and of all the individual "Front Porch" sessions.

I thought, "Is this really real? Are we really marching in this Parade?"

I peeped out the side of my eyes and saw all of the colored faces lining each side of the sidewalks and on the edge of the streets. As they shouted. I could hear joy, happiness, and enthusiasm in their voices. I could see pride and elated self-worth in their eyes. I could feel the strength and encouragement illuminating from their black bodies. "Yes, they are our kids, March on Children".

The main portion of the parade, the floats, and all of the white bands, had passed ahead us, and the rodeo cowboys and who ever rode a horse were way ahead of us.

Yes, you guessed it! We were marching in "horse manure", but I saw colored folks who were jumping, yelling, waving, and shouting out our names. "Look, there's Andrew", "Blow that horn Connie", "Look at Harold beat that drum". "Wow, will you look at Clarence step!"

There were Little Colored Children running along by the side of the band, imitating playing instruments and our marching steps. Little Colored Boys and Girls who in years to come would be marching in a Sebring Christmas Parade...marching and wearing **real colorful blue and gold** uniforms. Little boys and girls were yelling and watching with glee, dreams and wonder, as we marched.

We were stepping high. We were **stepping over, around**, and **sometimes in horse manure**. But, we proudly marched on, and we played the only march we knew how, "Washington Post" over and over again. The entire colored community came out to cheer us on: the teachers, the preachers, the orange grove pickers, the tomato pickers, the cucumber and bean pickers, the shop owners, the dry cleaners, barbers and beauticians. The colored men who worked in white folk's yards came out dressed in their work clothes and housemaids, janitors, and garbage workers came in their uniforms.

They all cheered, for we were **a proud, joyful happy people**. **You see, we were making history: A colored band in a white Christmas parade!**

Chapter 12

A Summer To Remember

I remember the summer I turned thirteen years old because it was during this period that I learned what "Fight or Fright" really meant.

Several months before beginning the plans that would change my life, Dr. Weems told me that due to my asthma I would never be able to play sports games or run and be involved in strenuous activities which could cause an asthma attack.

Well, I was determined that I was going to play both basketball and football in high school and I began to think and plan how to accomplish this impossible feat.

I took a "Jim Atlas" clipping from a comic book and ordered flower seeds to sell in the neighborhood. By selling one hundred dollar's worth of seeds, I was rewarded with a weightlifting set (fifty pounds). Certainly, not much by today's standards, but that was enough weight for me at that time.

Before school was out in May, I had sold all of my flower seeds and was eagerly awaiting my weightlifting set.

I can remember the day I got that Express office notice that there was a package waiting for Robert Walker. I was so excited, but yet afraid that Mother or Dad would find out. They didn't want me to do anything that would bring on another Asthma attack, and lifting weights was out of the question. They both would have "skinned me alive" if they knew what I was about to do.

Anyway, I took my little red wagon and ran across town, over the railroad tracks that separated "colored town" from "white town", past the "white high school, past the "white drug store", around the "white circle park" and then to the Express office.

(The Circle Park was a small park. In the center of town that "colored folks" were not allowed to sit in or walk through, as a child growing up in Sebring I was chased out of the park several times.)

I loaded my weights on that little red wagon and, was that ever a job pushing and pulling that load back home! I don't' know how long it took me to get back to my house, but I knew that I couldn't bring those weights into or around the house where Mother, Dad or my little sister, Elaine, would see them. So, I hid them in the grapefruit grove behind our house. I put them in a "tractor shed" where Mr. Hunter kept the tractor he used when he sprayed the citrus trees.

Every day after school, I would hurry home and do my chores and then call out, "Hey, Ma! I'm going out back for a little while, OK?" When Mother agreed, I would go to the tractor shed and "work out" with my weights; I would also run through the grapefruit grove, up one row and down the other, Running in that thick white sand, running and lifting weights was building up my lungs, building up my muscles, and strengthening my heart. Oh, I remember so well, working out every day except Sunday. Sunday was a day of worship, from morning until night.

Finally, school ended and I continued to work out during the summer and my muscles got bigger, my breathing improved, and I had fewer asthma attacks. I learned about my body and health; I learned how to take care of myself, and I learned how to cover up at night and wear caps anytime I was outside at night. I was determined to play sports, my first year in Junior High School.

One day when I heard Mother calling: "Billy, Bobby, come here." I was out back eating an orange. Billy, my fourteen-year-old brother, was feeding corn to his NFFA project chickens.

Ma was calling, "Billy, Bobby, come on in this house." I looked up at the sun and from the way my stomach was growling, I knew it was almost noon and that meant "lunch" time. I also knew what Mother wanted with Billy and me.

You see, Daddy worked with Mr. Henry's "Lemon Street Beer Garden", which was a saloon where colored men and women would go to drink, shoot pool and dance. They even had a gambling parlor upstairs on the second floor.

It was time to take Daddy his lunch. I didn't mind this little chore. Infact, I liked it very much. This was the chance to see the women with their long black hair and short dresses, red lips and always smelling so good and sweet. I liked the way they would be dancing and moving with the men, dances like the "slow drag". I also liked the way they would pull me to their bosom, hug me real close and look at my Dad and say, "Charlie you better watch this boy, he's getting these big muscles, beginning to look like "Joe Louis".

I remember the smell of that old saloon…beer, cigarette smoke, whiskey, perfume and sweat. Oh, how I like it! I can still see the old rainbow colored jukebox and hear the music which was usually old blues records, by Howling Wolf, Little Willie Johnson, T. Bone Walker, Bessie Smith, Harmonica Slim or Slim Hopkins. That kind of blues you don't hear any more.

Also there was Billy Holiday, Louis Armstrong on trumpet, Louis Jordan on Sax, Billie Eckstein, and Billy Daniels, real popular musicians. It was by these frequent trips to the beer joint carrying Dad's lunch and being on Lemon Street that I learned to love and appreciate Blues and Jazz music.

Now, as I said, I didn't mind going to the beer joint on Lemon Street, but there was a problem getting to Lemon Street. In fact, there were several problems, namely, the

Kelsey Boys, the Hays Boys and the empty lots with weeds and bushes.

K. B. and B.J. the "two Giants" that lived on Highlands Avenue, and Albert, Freddie and Cabbie Hays, the "Missile throwing kids" of Harris Street were specific problems.

K. B. and B.J. were sons of the colored landscaper. Both were large, ugly boys whose primary reason for living was to beat up on other kids and up to this summer, Billy and I were two of their favorite kids to beat. I swear, those two guys would hide in the bushes or up in the trees, waiting for Billy or me to come on Highlands Avenue just so that they could beat us and take our money, marbles, food, etc.

It didn't matter why, they would beat us sometime just for the fun of it and chase us home. The only time Mother or Dad would interfere was when they would come into the yard. I would talk plenty of trash then, because I knew Mother would come out of the house with the broom and chase them away.

The other nightmare was the Hays boys. They were about our size, but then they were Fierce Fierce and in addition to the three older boys, "there was about a hundred little ones". (Actually there were only four little ones) They would hang out at the corner of Harris and Lemon Streets and ambush kids as they passed on their way to Spooner's Grocery Store. They would throw bottles, cans, rocks, tree limbs, tree stumps, anything they could get their hands on, and they were pretty accurate. Billy and I got a lot of lumps and cuts from the various missiles they would throw at us as we tried to enter Lemon Street.

Then, of course, the other problem or obstacle in getting to Lemon Street was the open field, empty lots, with hot, very hot sand, palmetto palms, bushes, weeds filled with sandy spurs and occasionally a black snake or pygmy rattlesnake. Billy and I did not challenge the jungle often, of course. [Now, the lots have been cleared and houses have been built,] but back then, it was a real scary jungle and not many neighborhood kids would dare venture into that area, unless it was absolutely necessary.

That particular day, Billy and I decided we were not going to go around the long way via Harris Street and stand the chance of getting hit with flying missiles by the Hays boys. Neither did we feel up to running through the empty lots in that hot sand, getting stickers all over us. Therefore, it meant going through the Kelsey boys...

They must have seen us as we came off the front porch and turned east, heading towards Highlands Avenue, because when we got to Highlands, there they were waiting and looking like King Kong and company. K. B. was a foot taller than Billy, who was nearly six feet tall. Therefore, he was sure enough a giant to me. I was many inches shorter than Billy, but by then I was real husky and strong from lifting weights and exercising. B.J. was also taller then either Billy or I was, but slimmer and lanky.

K.B. spoke first, "Gotcha old man's food, huh? Gimme a looksee." Billy didn't say a thing. He just put the lunch bucket on the ground and the next thing I knew he was tackling K.B. I didn't need another cue; I ran into B.J. with my head down, picked him up and threw him to the ground. I got on top of him with my knees on his arms, and started punching him in the face, nose, mouth, and head...anywhere I could land a lick. He was yelling and screaming, and I was saying "Don't you ever bother me again. You hear? You had enough? Do you give?"

He finally managed to say, "I give" loud enough to hear, but by that time blood was everywhere; his nose was bleeding, lips were bloody and swollen. My fist was bruised and I was so mad I was crying as I was hitting him.

I glanced over to see what had happened to Billy and K. B. I saw K. B. on the ground holding his stomach. He was groaning and Billy was telling him, "Don't you ever bother me again or I'll give you some more. Do you hear me, K. B.?"

I remember K. B. nodding his head, he was still groaning too. Later I discovered that Billy had rammed him with his head and hit him several times in the stomach. K. B. was so tall I guess Billy couldn't reach his head. In any case, we licked the Kelsey Giants that day and from that day on they were no longer Giants, just tall humble kids, and they never bothered us again.

In fact, word about us Walker boys beating the Kelsey boys spread throughout colored town. The Hays boys heard about us too and later in the week when Billy and I decided to go to Spooner's Store on Harris and Lemon Streets we didn't even see the Hays boys. I can't imagine them not being on that corner, could be they were hiding from us. How about that!

That summer was a growing-up time for me; my weight lifting had paid off. I was a real husky boy of soon to be 13 years old, and I could run faster and longer after training in the orange and grapefruit groves.

Hurry up, seventh grade, I was ready for school to start. I was ready to play Junior High football and basketball. You know the best part, Mother and Dad never knew what came over their little sickly boy, but their prayers were answered. I was cured from asthma and later became a four-letter athlete in high school, but that's another story in *The Way Things Were.*

Chapter 13

The Bike Ride

"Billy, Bobby, it's time to get up", that's my dad on his way to the bathroom. He is up every morning at 6 A. M. sharp, every morning except on Sunday, that is. However, on Sundays he allows us to sleep until Mother calls us for breakfast and family prayer.

But this is not Sunday, in fact, it is Saturday morning, and little did Dad know that I had been awake since two or three A.M. In fact, I really didn't get too much sleep, being that I was so excited and "pumped up" for The Bike Ride.

I was twelve years old and on August 7, I would be thirteen years old. Summer had already brought about some big changes in my life. I was secretly lifting weights and getting stronger. I was running and doing exercises which were helping me to lose weight also.

Earlier in the summer my brother, Billy and I had fought the Kelsey brothers (K.B. and B.J.) and K.B. and Billy became friend. In fact, from that day onward through high school, B.J. became a very close pal of mine and we hung out together every chance we could get.

Back to that particular Saturday morning: "Bobby, why are you dressed so quick this morning? Billy usually beats you up", Dad asked me as he came out of the bathroom. I was ready to go in to wash my face, brush my teeth and manage other regular body functions.

"Charlie, I told you last night about Bobby and the boys' bike ride. You done forgot already?" Mother was trying to remind Dad as she busily prepared breakfast.

As Mother explained "things" to Dad, I busied myself getting all my "stuff" together. My back pack would carry a blanket, pocket knife, flashlight, towel, soap, can opener, water canteen, and the lunch that Mother was making for me. (Bologna and cheese sandwiches, peanut butter crackers and two Babe Ruth candy bars, which were seven inches long and only cost five cents.)

Pretty soon Billy and Elaine were up out of bed and we were all sitting down for a Saturday breakfast. That's when I got the chance to tell everybody about "The Bike Ride". So I said, "During the last month in school, my sixth grade class took a field trip to Highlands Hammock Park with our teacher, Miss Mayo. We had such a great time, that some of my male classmates talked about coming back to Highlands Hammock.

Dad was sopping syrup with a hot buttered biscuit when he asked, "What boys are you talking 'bout?"

I answered, "classmates Pops Jenkins, Connie Shoates, Benjamin Mays, John Ben, Spencer and Robert Burgess and Alfred Cooper. We've been talking about it for several weeks and decided that since we all had bikes and were very good riders, why not pack a picnic lunch and ride out to Highlands Hammock on our bikes. A great idea, right!" I looked around the table to see if anybody was as excited as I was. Elaine said, "I wanna go".

I just ignored her and looked at Billy. He said, "You guys are crazy. You'll be dead tired-falling off your bikes before you git to Harder Hall, and that's a lot closer than Highlands Hammock."

"Bobby, that is a rather far ride. I know, because I walk out that way to work for Mr. Piety and he lives near Harder Hall." Mother looked at me with deep concern, but I was watching my dad's face to see what his expression was saying. I didn't see any wrinkles in his brow. In fact, he didn't say anything while he was sopping his syrup with another biscuit; but when he was finished he looked at me then at Mother, then back to me and said, "You be back home before 5 P.M., you hear!"

I finished drinking my milk and said, "Excuse my seat" and went out doors to get ready.

By 9 A.M. we were all gathered around at Connie Shoates` house on Tangerine Street. All seven of us, with our bikes, back packs, sandwiches, soda pops, caps, blankets and water canteens. We even had a stick with a red handkerchief tied to it. Alfred Cooper decided to tie the stick to his bike. We read or heard somewhere that Bike Riders were supposed to carry a flag of some sort to warn car traffic.

"Hey man, let's git started, it's gitting hot as the devil already", said Ben.

"Yea! Last one out to Highlands Hammock is a rotten egg", I yelled, as I started to fast peddle and got the lead on everybody. Pretty soon we were started down Highland

Avenue heading toward Kenilworth Avenue and then around the Fairground Field approaching Kenilworth Hotel on South Ridgewood Drive!

We could see the white golfers and colored caddies at the Kenilworth Golf Course, so we slowed down to talk with "Bro Boy", "Pop", "Simon", and "Alfonzo", a few boys who were in the "Caddie Pen" waiting for the caddy master to call their names. (The caddie pen was a small fenced area for the caddies to wait until they were called to caddy)

When their name was called they would go up to the club house and get the golf bag for the "white" golfer and carry it while he played golf. None of us were large enough to caddy at that time, but we sometimes would "shad balls". (Pick up the balls for the "white" golfer, who was practicing hitting the ball. This usually paid from one to four dollars depending on how long and how many balls the golfer hit.)

"Cumon, ya'll, we got a long way to go", called Alfred, and all of us got to peddling fast, before I said, "Hey, slow down, fore we burn out". We then fell in line, one behind the other, me leading and Alfred bringing up the rear.

While we were riding we would occasionally start a song, "row, row, row your boat, gently down the stream." This would last until someone would start another song. Occasionally when a car passed us someone would blow their horn, or some would yell, "Hey, you niggers where you going?" or "You black monkeys better git off the road before ya'll git kilt."

We knew not to say anything back to the voice that insulted us or even to look in the direction of the voice. We knew better, but Ben was real sensitive and mean and he started yelling back, "You white cracker". I thought sure the truck would stop and the white people would git after us, but they didn't.

"Ben, you know better than that, just ignore dem dommies. Cumon up wid me," I said. I was afraid Ben would get us tarred and feathered before we even got to Jackson Lake. The rest of them let Ben ride directly behind me for the rest of the trip.

About 10.30 A.M. we were at Harder Hall Golf Course. We stopped to drink a soda and talk with some other colored boys who were at the caddy shack waiting to go caddying to make some money. Kenilworth Lodge and Harder Hall were the only two Golf Courses where a colored man or boy could caddy and make ten to twenty dollars a day and that was "good Pay' during the 1950's. In fact not too many jobs were available for a colored man other than picking fruit.

A colored lady called Ma Lucy had a little sandwich shop near the caddy house and she sold sodas. (Grapette, Strawberry, Royal Crown, Root Beer, Orange and Coca Cola) One could buy a sandwich and a soda for fifty cents. (Forty cents for the sandwich and ten cents for the soda) Usually a soda was only five cents, but I guess Miss Lucy decided she had to make a little extra…some folks said she was taking 'vantage of the caddie's cause they be hot, hungry and had nobody else to buy from and nowhere else to eat. (Back in the fifties, there was no such thing as McDonalds, Burger King, Hardies, Kentucky Fried Chicken or Windy's in that little southern town.)

We left Harder Hall about 11 A.M. and started again to Highland Hammock Park. The more we rode, the hotter it got and our little legs were getting tired. Finally we saw a sign that read "Highlands Hammock Park straight ahead five miles. Wow, we still had a long way to go.

We decided to stop under a tall oak tree with moss hanging down and take a break. That's when Pop said, "You know what, fellows" I for one would rather just ride on around the lake and go back home".

"Yea, it's almost 12 noon and us ain't even there", said Spencer, "and when we git there we won't have time to do nuttin but turn 'round and come back". I was thinking to myself that I had to be home by five P.M.

So we talked, took out our sandwiches, and before long we were having a picnic under the big oak tree on the side of the road about five miles from our destination…and yes, you guessed it. We layed up under that big old oak tree, and talked and dozed; and before long, a whole hour had passed.

"Fellows, I got to be home by 5 P.M. or my dad gonna skin me alive". I started cleaning up my mess, getting my bike ready. Connie followed my example and said, "Why don't we take the short cut to around Jackson Lake, that way we don't have to go back the long way we came."

Robert J. Walker (Bobby)

We all agreed. And to this day, I can't understand why I thought going around Jackson Lake would be a short cut. Maybe it's because we had only been around Jackson once or twice before. In fact, I don't think Ben or Pop had ever been around Jackson Lake. Anyway, we started riding and before long our little legs began to get tired again and we stopped under another shady tree near what is now called "Veterans Beach Park."

Little did we know at that time, but what appeared to be a short cut by going around Jackson Lake, turned out to be a "big miscalculation." You see, there were several bends and curves that were hidden from our eyes. Since Connie Shoates and myself were the only ones who had been around the entire lake (and that was while riding in a car) we couldn't imagine how long those curves were and the miles they added to "the short cut".

Alfred said, "I'm about done in and I'm thirsty; Bobby, Gimme a drink". I shook my canteen; it was empty! "I'm out, ask Pop for some." We all looked at Pop who shrugged his shoulders, "Man, I ain't gone none neither."

100

Spence started cursing and swearing, "Yall" done drunk up all de ***%$@** water! Now what we gonna do!" (Spence learned to cuss from listening to men on corner who were drinking moonshine and wine)

I jumped on my bike and started peddling. Soon, the rest of the fellows started riding too. But, we were no longer a team. We were no longer laughing and riding wildly, jockeying for position, or even joking with each other. We were reserving all of our energy. The sun was getting hotter and hotter. We didn't ride like friends or pals out for a fun bike ride, we were like strangers…nobody talking. We were all strung out, separated from each other, struggling, and pumping our little legs as much as we could.

At one point, I looked back behind me, Alfred was directly behind me, but Connie was walking and pushing his bike; Spencer and Robert Burgess were wobbling and weaving; Ben and Pop were way, way back, just barely creeping along. And I was soooo tired, I thought to myself, "we're gonna be in trouble."

The sun was getting hotter. We were tired, thirsty and "the short way' was a whole lot longer than we had thought.

Then I remember looking up at this big white house with palm trees and oak trees in the front yard. We had been riding on the roadside near the lake, but this house was on the other side.

To this day, I don't know what propelled me across that street (Lakeview Drive) to the other side but the next thing I recall, I was standing at the front door of that big white house ringing the door bell and knocking on the door. (Remember, this was sometime around 1950-51 in a small southern city located in Central Florida.)

I must have ring that bell several times and was still knocking when the front door was suddenly pulled open and a tiny white lady yelled, "By Gosh", What ya'll want ringing on my front door for? Why ain't you at the back doah? Now git...git I say."

"But Mam", I stutter. "I wwwant ", but before I could say any more she yelled out again. "Lordy Mercy, there's more of `em coming up the walkway."

By that time, Alfred and Connie was pushing their bikes up the walkway, and as I turned to go around to the back door, I could see the rest of the fellows struggling up the road near the big white house.

When I got around to the back door, the little old lady was standing there behind the screen door peeping out at me. "Whatcha want?" she asked. I said, "Miss White Lady, me and my buddies was out bike riding and we ran out of water. Could we please have a drink?"

She said, "Now first thing, don't ya'll know no better than to be coming up in my walkway at the front door?" But before I could answer her she added, "look at ya'll, all sweaty and dirty." Ben was near the back yard water hose and said, "Could I git a drink, Miss White Lady?" She finally came all the way out the door and wiped her face with a white towel and just stood there with one hand on her hip, wiping her face. Finally, she asked "How far, ya'll come?"

Connie spoke up, "Miss Lady we rode from home across the tracks to almost Highlands Hammock then to here. We been riding since 9 A.M."

I was waiting for her to do one of two things: Tell us to get off her property or tell us to go ahead and drink from the back yard faucet. BUT, she did something that to this very day I'll never forget. I guess that's why I can still write about it.

She said, "Ya'll wait here". Then she went back into the house and we all came together on the back porch. We could hear her in the kitchen pulling cabinet doors open and closing them. We could hear jars clinking together. We looked at each other and wondered what was going on. Then we heard the icebox opening and then the ice pick hitting ice, then water running from the kitchen faucet.

After what seemed like hours, and our lips were parched and cracked, white and dry, the door opened and this little white lady stood there with a large breakfast tray. On it were seven pint jars filled with cold "ice" water. Needless to say, each of us had our own jar to drink from.

For about twenty minutes, we kept that little old white lady pretty busy running in and out of that kitchen getting fresh water from the kitchen faucet.

We said our "thank yous" and our "goodbyes" to that good, kind old white lady. I don't' remember what time we finally got home that day. I can't even remember what my dad said about me coming home late. I do know that we told everybody in colored town and in school about the "good old white lady" who gave us the sweetest water we had ever drunk. To this very, day I can still taste the peaches that must have been in those "pint jars" that the little old lady poured out in a bowl, then let us drink water from the jars, rather than from her glasses. But then, maybe she just didn't have enough glasses for all of us.

I've asked myself that question for over fifty years. Why did she give us those jars? But regardless, that little old white lady was a God-sent White Angel who gave seven little colored boys "the sweetest water" they had ever tasted. You know what? I can still taste those peaches whenever I think about that day so long ago when "That was the way things were."

Chapter 14

A Friend Called Junior

It was a hot summer afternoon in 1952, and we were back in Millen, Georgia visiting Grandpa Alfred and Grandma Susie. The afternoon sun was going down behind the hill at our backs as Billy and I stood in the middle of a red clay road. We were looking eastward, and could barely make out the shape of a boy leading some cows.

"Junior, hey Junior", Billy was calling and I was jumping up and down waving my arms. "Junior, Junior," I yelled.

"I know that's Junior, and he's leading the cows back to the barn for the night", I said. "Yea, but he can't hear us," Said Billy; and he let go with a sharp whistle that cut through Grandpa's pecan orchid down across the trout creek, over the top of the tall pine trees, through Grandma's peanut garden to the open pasture, where hogs were rooting up the ground looking for earth worms, and finally ended up in Junior's ear under a wide straw hat.

It seemed like several seconds passed before he looked toward our direction, took his hat off and waved. Then he did something that made it certain he had seen and heard us. He took his fist and cupped them together and blew between the thumbs. It's called "blowing your fists" and Junior had taught Billy and me how to blow our fists many summers before, probably in 1947. We heard the clear sound come across the opening pasture, back over the tall pine trees, through Grandma's peanut garden, over the trout creek, through Grandpa's pecan orchid to our eagerly waiting ears. He had signaled that he saw us.

Now he knew that the Walker boys were back from for the summer visiting our grandparents. We often came to visit our Grandparents especially during the summer...sometimes for a couple of weeks or a month. This time we were spending the entire summer.

I was fourteen years old and would be fifteen in August. Billy was already sixteen years old with hair growing on his top lip, under his arms and other places where grown men had hair.

I was excited about visiting Millen, Georgia this particular summer because I had grown a whole lot since last summer and I was eager to show off my slick hair style, dark shades and sharp city clothes.

Junior Jenkins was a seventeen-year-old farm boy who had lived on the farm all of his life, but he was "cool" and crazy. We liked him a whole lot; he was fun and kept us involved in something all summer long. We learn a whole lot each summer by being around Junior. That's right, after seeing Junior, Bill and I talked long into the night about the things we were going to tell Junior the next day.

Around twelve noon the next day, Friday, Junior was in the front yard blowing his fist signaling for us to come outside. Soon we were slapping each other's hands in greetings. Junior had grown also and was a head taller then I, but about the same height as Billy, who at sixteen was almost six feet tall. We sat on the front-porch swing talking and exchanging stories about what happened since we last saw each other.

Junior had an eighteen-year-old sister named Evelyn. Their mother had married Deacon Jenkins after their real

Daddy had left the country and moved to Philadelphia, Pennsylvania. Deacon and Mrs. Jenkins were good decent folks, who were Grandpa and Grandma's closest friends.

There were several colored farmers in the general area called "Possum Heights". Each farm consisted of about seventy-five to one hundred acres of farmland. Both Deacon Jenkins and Grandpa Walker had more than seventy-five acres because they had two or more mules. Curiously, one mule was needed to farm fifty acres of land.

It was Grandpa who taught us how to pick cotton, pull corn, pull watermelons and plow behind the mules. But it was Junior who made the work fun. In fact, it seems like Junior was always smiling or laughing. I must have known Junior since I was seven years old, up until I was fifteen years old and I don't even remember seeing Junior angry or sad.

That first morning, we left the family front porch and started walking toward the Jenkins. "Hey, you guys wanna drink some wine? Come on, let's go to the barn". We followed Junior to the barn and soon we were laying back on bails of hay and drinking blackberry wine made from blackberries. I could hear Evelyn getting water from the well at the same time Junior said, "Come on, let's go check the mail." Junior said, "Let's sing songs and each drink from his own jug."

We each got a jug of wine and went out the side barn door drinking and feeling mellow. I was floating and feeling good when suddenly I realized that Billy was not walking with us. "Hey Junior, where's Billy?" I asked. Junior replied, "Oh, Bobby, don't worry about Billy. He is probably too drunk, can't hold his liquor." But even as Junior spoke, somehow he didn't sound convincing, but I soon forgot about Billy as we walked, it took around about an hour to walk down to the four-way crossing.

Where the roads intersected, mail boxes were on each side of the road so the mailman would come and place the mail for farms in that area. We checked the mail box for Deacon Jenkins and found several letters and magazines and a Sears Roebuck catalog. We sat there looking through the magazines when my stomach started to growling and my head started swirling and before I knew anything I had thrown up all of my breakfast.

Junior laughed, jumping up and down, "You get sick off a little wine! Boy, what you gonna do when you get hold of some "shine"?

"Come on, Junior, let's go back. I need to wash up in some cold water." In fact, I was hot, sweaty, sick and wanted to take a whole bucket of well water and throw it on my head. I started back up the road and Junior reluctantly followed.

"Hey, Bobby, slow down, boy, you gonna make yourself sicker."

I didn't think so, I just wanted to get some cold water on my head and sit down in the cool barn or under a nice big shady pecan tree. It was close to twelve noon and getting "Georgia hot".

The faster I tried to walk the more excuses Junior would have to slow me down. "Come here, look at the this hawk's nest" or "there goes a rabbit trail." One time I looked back and Junior was on his knees peeping into some bushes and wanting me to come see.

"Don't make any noise", he whispered as he pointed through the bushes at a small patch of leaves. As I bent forward, I could see two reddish brown necks of two little birds, their mouths were wide open, eyes closed, making little squawks.

"Common, Junior, let's get out of here before the mama bird comes back. I'm sick to my stomach already, I don't need to get sick to my head too." "Oh, man ain't no mama bird gonna show up with me here." About that time we both heard the callings of the blue jay birds and in a few minutes they were all around us diving at our heads. Junior and I started running, but blue jays were coming at us from every direction. Those birds chased us all the way back to the barn.

I came through the barn and went to the well and drew up some cool water. I took a small drink and then poured the whole bucket full over my head.

Junior yelled, "Save a drink for me." I told him, "Draw your own water, smarty. I told you to leave them birds alone. I knew that mother bird was around somewhere." I left Junior drawing another bucket of water and walked around to the front of the house. Just then Billy was coming out of the house onto the front porch.

"Hey, Billy, what you do man, get drunk and pass out? Hey, Junior, one little drink of wine and Billy fall out?" I was trying to pick on him and make fun of him. I finally had something to laugh about my big brother. He couldn't drink one swig of wine. But then, as I looked into Billy's face, he looked like he was in a daze. He went and sat on the swing and and just stared out into the yard.

I tried talking to him but he didn't appear to hear anything I was saying. I went to the front door and could see Evelyn moving around inside. I went into the parlor room and saw Evelyn straightening the blanket on the sofa and she too had a strange little smile on her face and a twinkle in her eyes.

She said, "Hey, Bobby ya'll made it back. Did we get any mail?" "Yea," I told her, "Junior got it". I went back outside on the porch and looked real hard at my brother's face. Yes, he too had that same type of little smile on his face and a little twinkle in his eye.

He sat on the porch swing and leaned back with his hand behind his head and just sort of stared off into space like I wasn't even there.

Something happened to Billy that day, something real important, but it was almost twenty years later before Billy told me the details. But then that was the summer when many exciting events took place.

Both Billy and I learned a whole lot from being around Junior that summer. Oh, so much more to write about in *The Way Things Were.*

Chapter 15

Mother Goes To College

It was really hot that summer of 1953. In fact, it was one of the hottest summers of my life, mainly because Daddy had me working all summer long. He didn't send us to Millen, Georgia to stay with Grandpa during the summer as was our custom. In fact, it seems like we were working every day that summer doing something to earn money for school clothes. We did jobs like cutting lawns, picking beans, caddying at the golf course, picking oranges, cutting down palm trees, or repairing lawn mowers.

Billy and I were growing boys, soon to be men and Dad was teaching us the value of hard work and earning an honest dollar. Whatever way there was to earn an honest dollar the Walker family was doing it.

Mother and Elaine were washing white folks clothes. Back then they called it "taking in laundry" for the "good white folks". Some days Mother would do house cleaning.

I remember some times the white lady would drive Mother to and from work in her long black car and then other times Mother would walk to the white lady's house. Sometimes she had to walk all the way back home.

....

In 1973 during a return visit to Sebring, Mother and I were just riding around the city one-day. She pointed out the homes of the white folks where she had worked and the distances she had walked, often ten to twelve miles round trip.

....

That summer of 1953, we worked particularly hard. Daddy picked oranges during the day and was night manager at Mr. Henry's beer joint and club. He also found time to clean the Gilbert's Drug Store down town on the Circle.

It was sometime in late August 1953 that Mother and Dad called us children to the dinning room table for a family meeting.

Mother told us that she was going back to college to get her B.S. degree. She said that she and Daddy had been planning and waiting for us children to get big enough to be responsible and be able to "keep house" and to manage ourselves in a proper manner.

Mother stated that she and Daddy had taught us how to take care of ourselves, like how to cook, bake, wash clothes, iron clothes, clean the house clean the yard; we knew how to sew and mend our clothes. We knew how to take care of the chickens and our garden as well as how to take care of each other. We knew how to pray, how to attend Sunday school and church. We knew how to love and support each other...they had taught us so very well!

Mother said that it was time for her to go get that B. S. degree so that she could teach school and help Daddy financially. Our mother had vision!

She was a praying, God fearing woman, who loved God and taught each of us the value of prayer and establishing a personal relationship with God.

Mother and Dad directed and assisted us in making a chore schedule:

-Bobby would cook breakfast Monday through Friday. In the afternoon I had to stay after school for football or basketball practice.

- Elaine would cook dinner Monday through Friday.

- Billy would clean house each afternoon before going to his job at night to the movie theater.

- We rotated on the week-end cooking meals, but we all worked together to clean the house and the yard on Saturday. On Sunday we attended Sunday school and morning church services...afternoon it was BYPU and evening services on the second and fourth Sundays.

....

September 1953 Mother went to Bethune Cookman College in Daytona Beach, Florida. She graduated in 1956-57 and later earned a masters degree at Florida A. & M. She taught school in Highlands County for thirty years and was selected as the Teacher of The Year on four different occasions. In 1977 she received the community award for

Leadership in Education at the annual Distinguished Service Award Ceremony sponsored by the Sebring News and the Greater Sebring Chamber of Commerce. Several years later Mother was selected "Mother of The Year" for Highlands County and was one of the runners up as the State of Florida "Mother of The Year".

I thank God for my mother and father and I remember it so well that evening in 1953 when Mother called us around the dinning room table and announced, "I am going back to college!" And that's another chapter in *The Way Things Were*.

Chapter 16

Falsely Accused

The school year 1953-54 and I was in the tenth grade. The reason I can remember so well is that Mr. Hudson had a brand new 1953 red and black Chevrolet car.

Most of us fellows in high school thought Mr. Hudson was real cool. He didn't look much older than we did and he was a real classy dancer and wore his hair in the latest hairstyle…"the bush". (The front hair is high and gradually slopes low toward the back.)

I was rather popular in high school because I was the football quarterback and a starting point guard on the basketball team. I was muscular and a smooth talker with the girls. In fact, I though I was "Mr. Cool".

On this particular school day, Mr. Hudson allowed me and another football star called John, to use his car to go to a grocery store down town to get discarded vegetables for the school's agricultural rabbit project. Well, since it was near the last period of school several other fellows wanted to ride to town with us. And, unknown to Mr. Hudson, we said "O.K." Simian and Willie joined us as we piled into the new car with John driving.

Now did I mention this is the year 1953 in mid May in a little southern Florida City called Sebring?

`We picked up the old discarded vegetables and put them in the trunk of the car. Then Simian made this "great suggestion", "Hey man, we got this mean machine for the next hour, why not go for a ride around Lake Jackson?"

I think it's a great idea and tell John to "hit the gas". We head up Pine Street to Ridgewood Drive and turn left heading toward the "Circle" and that's where trouble is waiting.

As we approached to go around the Circle a group of white girls were coming through the Circle Park and some of them came directly out in front of the car telling us to stop. Of course, we stopped until they all (twenty or more) had taken their slow sweet time crossing the street laughing and calling us names as they pointed and poked fun at the little "N" boys...

Now what do you do in 1953 in the deep south? You do nothing but grin, lower your eyes, show your teeth and hold your temper!!!

We never did get to ride around Lake Jackson, instead we came back to E. O. Douglas campus, parked Mr. Hudson's car in his parking space and took the rabbit food to the agricultural building.

I was in my last hour class when the white uniformed policeman came into the band room and asked for me. I couldn't imagine what it was that he wanted with me; but after handcuffing me and leading me outside, I noticed several other policemen leading black boys to patrol cars. It looked like the whole Sebring Police Department was in E. O. Douglas campus just rounding up black boys from every class.

We were all taken to the principal's office. Mr. Nixon, the principal, was told that some "N" boys had tried to kidnap some white girls who were going swimming down to the city pier; and that these "N" boys had long hair up front and were driving a black and red Chevrolet car. We were guilty of being "black and driving a new car."

It looked like we were the guilty party. The white girls not only called us names, insulted us, embarrassed us, and now it appeared they were out to "kill us". For that's what white men did to black men or boys who even looked at their white women.

Did I forget to mention that these white girls crossing the street from the Circle Park were on their way to swimming classes down at the Sebring city pier and during that time 1950-1956 the city Circle Park and the city pier were off limits to coloreds, when I was in school.

I don't recall too much more after the policeman took my cuffs off and put me in a caged patrol car to take me downtown. I do recall "something" telling me to comb my hair and don't be afraid, don't cry, don't smile, don't say anything and don't do anything but obey the policeman.

The policeman drove me to the white high school and stopped outside a rear door near the gymnasium. He told me to stick my head out of the window. He waited a moment, which I did, then he drove off and started yelling at me, "You're a dead "N", "Don't you know we kill black men for bothering our ladies! We tar and feather little black boys for getting fresh with our girls". He continued this treatment all the way back up to the E. O. Douglas Campus.

After all of the black boys, about 14, were taken down, for what I later learned was, to be identified by the white girls, they couldn't identify any one. We then were told never again to come downtown between the hours of 2:30 to 3:30 P.M. You see, that was the time the white girls would dress in bathing suits and walk from the white high school gymnasium through the Circle Park down to the city pier for swimming classes. Black males, men and boys were not allowed to look at a white woman in a bathing suit. Yes, that's The Way Things Were in a little southern city called Sebring, Florida in the year 1953.

Note: The year is 2001 and I have retired and moved back to Sebring, Florida. I spend many afternoons sitting on a bench in the Circle Park, feeding the squirrels, listening to the birds singing, and watching cars and people passing by. I daydream and remember the days and times long ago when a "little colored boy" wasn't allowed to...

Chapter 17

The Price of Disobedience

The 1954-55 school year, I was in the 11th grade at E. O. Douglas School, which consisted of grades one through twelve for colored children during the era of segregation. The school was located in a little southern tourist town called Sebring in Central Florida.

As I recall that particular year of my life it was a really exciting time; a time for teenage love affairs, souped-up cars and athletic achievements. I Was "The Man". In fact, I was maturing rapidly every day, and learning more about the world around me...social, civic and economic situations.

My earlier years of "weight training" and "strenuous conditioning exercise" program had paid off. I was in excellent physical condition and the star player on the high school basketball and football teams.

Dad purchased a green 1948 Pontiac for me to drive. He told me that it was my responsibility to maintain the car and keep oil and gas in it at all times. I managed to do this by caddying on the local golf courses at Kenilworth Lodge and Harder Hall and working with Mr. Thomas who had a nursery business. I mowed laws, trimmed hedges and cut down trees. It was hard work, but it was better than going to the orange grove to pick fruit.

My Dad (Charlie Walker) worked three different jobs during that time; you see, my mother, Anna Bell Walker, had gone back to college to get her B. A. degree in order to teach school and help my Dad out with household expenses.

We three Walker children had worked out a household routine, which helped to maintain order in the Walker's household.

Billy, (oldest child) had graduated the previous year and was attending Tuskegee College in Tuskegee, Alabama. Elaine and I continued on with the routine of house cleaning, cooking, washing, ironing, baking, sewing, mowing, etc. Whatever chore needed to be done, we did it. Elaine and I knew our place, or purpose and our duties as Charlie and Anna Walker's children.

Now let me get to the primary story. It was sometime in November and our football team was having a great season with a record of 10-1, losing only to Dunbar School in Bartow, Florida. Now we were preparing for the Homecoming Game against Haines City, Florida.

Now for some reason that I have never been able to understand, students from the colored school (E. O. Douglas) in Sebring were not allowed to use the white school's football field. However, nearby Avon Park (white) High School allowed us to play our Homecoming Game on their "State of the Art" Football Field with night lights and bleachers on both sides of the field.

In fact, colored people were also allowed to attend the white theater in downtown Avon Park, but were not allowed to go to the white theater in downtown Sebring...I never could understand the reason for the restriction. (I often wonder why Avon Park white people were different from Sebring white folks.)

In any case, that's where the Homecoming Game was to be played "Under the bright night lights!" Wow! I couldn't wait to get out on that beautiful football field and play on real green grass with good upright goal posts, scoreboard and loud speakers. This game was real big time and everybody was expecting and looking forward to E. O. Douglas High School beating Haines City's football team.

Usually E. O. Douglas games were played on Saturday during the day, on a football field on Tangerine Street, that was a former cow pasture. The field was marked off with wet lime and white paint. There were no goal posts nor were there any bleachers. The people who came out to watch the games either brought their own chairs or used fruit crate boxes as seats.

Remember that this was in 1954-55 and segregation, prejudices and racial hostility existed openly. During this period of time most teams of southern colored schools played basketball games on hard-packed red or yellow clay courts which were marked with white lime. The football fields were identical to the E. O. Douglas schools football field. Now that I think about it, since we didn't have goal posts, the "quarterback sneak" was a main play for two-pt. conversion points after we scored a touchdown.

Mr. Mose Stubbs was the football and basketball coach and Mr. Leroy Wallace was the assistant coach. We were having a great season! HenryAnderson was at his best running touchdowns from right halfback position. Herman Ranch and Billie Carter were alternating left halfbacks and Gene Ranch and John Love were alternating fullbacks. Allonso Bells and Robert Burns were right and left end respectively. I couldn't have asked for a better offence team. Morwood Hawthone played center, Simon Knight was right tackle, Bobby Mason left tackle, Big Richard Williams was right guard and Gene Butcher was left guard.

Yes, sir, We were a "mean machine" and were outscoring our opponents by twenty or more points each game.

"Walker, I want you to run the football the first half, just keep feeding Anderson and Carter or whoever is in left back position. During the second half we will get to the air. By then their team will be so tired and confused we should have it pretty easy."

"Yea! No Sweat, Coach. We gonna kick butt 'come Sat night!" I was bragging and walking around the locker room slapping hands with all my teammates. "Yea" we were yelling, jumping and hugging each other like we had already won the game. Instead, it was Friday afternoon and we had just finished a light workout without 'tards (uniforms). The coaches were giving us a little pep talk.

Coach Wallace said: "Everybody take a shower...and don't forget to go directly home after the homecoming rally tonight. I don't want nobody dragging out there on that field tomorrow night."

When I got home my sister Elaine had dinner on the table. She and I had our chores and other house responsibilities down to a routine. Since Billy was in college Elaine and I had to really work together in close harmony, cleaning the house, cooking meals, washing clothes shopping, etc. Daddy was still working three jobs and Mother was still at Bethune Cookman College with one more year to go.

"Daddy, may I go to the homecoming pep rally tonight?" Naw, she didn't. "Not my sister." I know Elaine didn't ask that question. She hardly ever wants to attend the rallies. Usually she would wait and go to the homecoming dance after the game.

I gave here my best "mean look" but she just grinned and continued. "I won't stay long. Bobby can bring me home early and go back if he wants to." (She knew she had messed up my plans.)

"Ha", I thought, "Like she's making it easy for me".

I said, "But Elaine, you know you don't like all that noise and rowdiness. It's gonna be a mess out there."

I looked at Dad and he was looking at Elaine. "You sure you want to go?" he asked. Elaine nodded, yes, and my goose was cooked!

"Bobby, you make sure you get Elaine home by 10 P.M., You hear!"

"Yes sir", I said. That was it…no Getting out of it. I was stuck with my baby sister!

The rally was up on "the hill" in the E. O. Douglas lunchroom, which was used for the auditorium, dance room and any other large assemblies. It was the largest room on campus. (This area now houses the Highlands County School Administration Office.)

Man, it was jamming, the music was blasting, and all my girls were there. I was having a good time, when Elaine tapped me on my shoulder and said, "It's time to go".

I didn't want to go. No way! I didn't want to leave Miss Helen, a little freshman girl who had just come over to E. O. Douglas from Hopewell Junior High in Avon Park. I had finally managed to get her up for a dance and I sure didn't want to take the chance of losing out with her.

I quickly looked around the dance floor to see if I could get somebody to take Elaine home.

"Hey, Teddie Ted Socket come here, Man, I got something I want you to do for me." I knew Teddie kinda liked my sister so I thought it would be easy to get him to drive Elaine home for me. I also knew he was a nice fellow. He came from a good family...The Sockets from DeSoto City. So I wasn't worried about him doing anything wrong. He also was on the football team and I trusted him.

"Sure, Bobby, I'll do that for you, and you be sure to throw a few passes my way on tomorrow night, O.K.?"

"Yea, Man I'll do just that. Now you take her straight home." Now that I reflect on that night so long ago, I don't remember Elaine objecting to the switch at all. In fact, I think she was grinning and smiling all the time, cause she kinda liked Teddie too.

I got home that Friday night a little bit after 11 P.M. Daddy wasn't home yet. He usually got home sometime around 1:30 A. M. after he closed the Edmond Henry Beer Joint.

I was asleep when I heard "Bobby, git up, boy. Bobby git out here". I didn't have to see the wrinkles in his forehead, his voice said it all. He was ANGRY!

"Where's your sister?" I immediately ran to Elaine's room and my heart was beating soooo fast. I tried to think what could have happened. I was so sure everything was O.K. so I didn't even check her room when I came home at 11 P.M.

"Man, that was dumb," I thought, "What did Teddie do? I'm gonna kill him." All kinds of thoughts were running through my head. When I got to Elaine's room, I found the light switch on, and...she was sleeping so soundly, with a smile on her face. I turned the light off and closed the door quietly...

"Daddy, she is in her room asleep." I looked at him for an explanation, wondering why was he so angry. She was home…safe asleep.

"Yea! I know she is home now at 1 P.M. but she wasn't home at 10.P.M. and she wasn't home at11 P.M. In fact, she didn't get home until after 12 midnight! AND YOU DIDN'T BRING HER HOME LIKE I TOLD YOU!"

I can't remember all the excuses I gave Dad that night. In fact, I can't even remember what Elaine told me what had happened. (something about a flat tire.) I can't remember how Dad knew Elaine wasn't home at 10 P.M. or 11 P.M. What I do remember are these words:

BOBBY, YOU DISOBEYED ME AND THAT REALLY DISAPPOINTS ME, SON. YOU'RE TOO BIG TO WHIP…THEREFORE…YOU WILL NOT PLAY IN THAT GAME TOMORROW. YOU WILL NOT GO TO THAT GAME TOMORROW. YOU WILL NOT LEAVE THIS HOUSE ON TOMORROW. AND YOU WILL NOT DRIVE YOUR CAR AT ALL NEXT WEEK TO SCHOOL, TO CHURCH, TO WORK, NOWHERE, IS THAT CLEAR?

"Yes, Sir." I said, and went back to my bedroom. I was in a daze. I kept hearing his voice over and over, "You will not play......" I did not sleep, but somehow the sun came up and it was Saturday. The day of the BIG HOMECOMING FOOTBALL GAME...THE HOME COMING PARADE, THE HOMECOMING DANCE AND VICTORY CELEBRATION...

Daddy must be kidding. Surly he knows the importance of this game and how important it was for me to play. After all, I was the "star quarterback". Surely he was punishing me by making a threat. So with that thought in mind, I got up and made breakfast (which was my chore). I made pancakes, sausage, bacon, hot coffee, milk and a few scrambled eggs, just in case he wanted some.

After breakfast, I washed the dishes, swept the floors, and took out the garbage. Then I went outside and sat on the front porch where Daddy could see how sad I was.

I kept waiting for Daddy to smile and say, "I hope you learned your lesson and I'm gonna lift your restriction." But he put his hat on and said, "I'm gonna go git a haircut. Ya'll take care of all ya'll chores and Bobby, don't you leave this house!"

Oh well, so much for wishful thinking. I went to clean my room and started taking the bed sheets of the bed. Normally Saturday was wash day, but the parade would be starting soon and Elaine was playing in the band. She was getting ready to go to the corner of Highlands Avenue and Lemon Street to catch the school bus where the band, floats and people were gathering for the parade at the schoolhouse.

I said goodbye to Elaine. She looked real pretty in her blue and gold uniform. The band had come a long way from the black pants and white shirt days.

"See ya, Bobby, Daddy will probably come get you before game time."

That's it! Daddy was going to make me wait and suffer, then he will come get me later on this afternoon and take me over to Avon Park. I sat down later on the front porch as soon as I heard the band playing.

I sat there and imagined the floats and cars. I could see the band stepping high; I could hear the band playing real good. The sound came down Highlands Avenue real good; I could hear the car horns blowing, people yelling, laughing, calling out names as they passed by. I could imagine the majorettes…Helen, Wilma, Marva, Nelly, Betty and the drum major, Clarence, twirling their batons.

I could imagine the NFA boys dressed in black and gold colors, marching under the big sign, NEW FARMERS OF AMERICA. (The white students had clubs in their schools also, but they were called FUTURE FARMERS OF AMERICA.) That's segregation for you…both clubs did the same thing, which was to teach young boys about agriculture, and raising live stock (pigs, rabbits, cows, and chickens). They also learned how to be carpenters and to grow fruit trees and vegetable gardens.

Every now and then, Slayton Mathews, the colored policeman, would turn his siren on as they turned onto Lemon, the main street in colored town. I could hear the people on the sides of the street starting to clap and yell out as the floats passed by.

I decided that I didn't want to hear any more. I went back to my bedroom, took my football uniform out and put it on my bed. I laid my shoulder pads, hip pads, knee pads, and elbow pads out…got a wash rag and started shinning the pads, making sure that there wasn't any dirt or grass stains showing. I got my football shoes out, added a little more black polish and buffed them with a shoeshine rag.

Man, they were really shining. Then I got a wrench and tightened the cleats again just to make sure. A good way to slip and fall while running was to have a loose cleat or have several cleats fall off while you are running. I didn't want that to happen.

Finally the parade was over. I heard a car drive up out front!

I ran to the door. Coach Stubbs was standing there along with Coach Wallace. "Elaine told me what happened this morning. Where's your Daddy? Maybe I can get him to change his mind."

"He said he was going to get a haircut, so maybe he's still up to Mr. Matthews barbershop."

Coach Wallace said, "You be ready. We will send somebody back for you." I was feeling good. It looked like I was going to play after all.

Later that afternoon around 4 P.M. Daddy came home. (Kick off time was 7 P.M., so I had plenty of time to get over to Avon Park.) I had made a few porkchop sandwiches and offered Daddy a little lunch, even though I knew that he probably had gotten something to eat up at Mrs. Mamie Jone's Café. He had been gone since morning, but I thought it sure wouldn't hurt for me to be extra nice.

"Daddy, I made some iced tea also, want a drink?"

Dad said, "Yea, Bobby". That's it. He is talking to me, maybe Coach Stubbs convinced Daddy to let me play.

When I brought him the iced tea, I looked into his face to see if there were any wrinkles in his forehead. I didn't see any. I was getting really excited. I waited for him to say the magic words. "YOU CAN PLAY", but he drank the iced tea and went out to sit down on the front porch.

Elaine came home all worn out from marching in the parade. "Bobby, the parade was great, did you hear us playing?"

"Yea, Elaine, I could hear ya'll real good"

"Bobby, did you leave me a little dinner?"

"Yea, it's on the stove. The tea is in the icebox. I already put ice in the tea, so you don't have to use anymore. That ice has to last until Monday."

"O.K., O. K., I know", Elaine said as she went to her bedroom to wash and change clothes.

I heard some car doors slamming and looked to see who was coming up onto the front porch...Mr. Nixon, the principal, Mrs. Jones, Mrs. Daniels and Mrs. Thomas (my homeroom teacher and class sponsor)!

Surely all of these big wheels could persuade Daddy...I tried to listen without being seen, but I could only hear bits and pieces of the conversation.

"Mr. Walker, you know how important this game is to the school..."

"Why, we could be recognized as AAA champions if we win this last game...and Bobby, will probably get more letters from colleges who will accept him on an athletic scholarship..."

I heard Mrs. Thomas clearly say, "I will be glad to keep him after school as some type of punishment and my husband, Edger, could work him cutting yards as extra punishment" On and on they talked.

I didn't hear anything from Dad. Not one word! But I am sure he was talking. Finally they all left at once. I heard the car doors slamming again, the engines starting up and cars leaving.

Silence. Just silence.

I expected Dad to call me to the front porch any moment. I expected him to put his arms around me and tell me how important I was to the team...the school...the community. I expected him to let me know what it would mean for E. O. Douglas to beat Haines City and become division triple A champions...but Silence. And more silence!

`Time passed. Before I knew it the yellow school bus had passed going up Highlands Avenue to the Lemon Street crossing. There the bus driver, Reverend Austin, would wait for the football team and cheerleaders. A second bus driven by Mrs. Branch would pick up the E. O. Douglas marching band and majorettes to take them to Avon Park.

Elaine said, "Daddy I'm getting ready to go." Then she peeked into my bedroom. I was lying down on the bed.

"Bobby, I'm so sorry. I wished I had never gone to that old pep rally. It's all my fault".

I looked up at her once again. She was all dressed up in her pretty band uniform. "Naw, Elaine, don't worry about it. You go have a good time and play good, O.K?" I gave her a hand slap and laid back down.

I heard her tell Daddy goodbye. Several minutes later, I heard Daddy walking around. I listened carefully...following his footsteps as he moved from the front porch to his bedroom, to the kitchen, to the bathroom, back to his bedroom.

I kept waiting for Daddy's booming voice to say, "Bobby, it's O.K. I am gonna let you play this time. I hope you learned your lesson. Don't you ever disobey me again, you hear!"

I kept waiting. I heard the car keys jingling as he picked them up and then...then...his footsteps were coming to the back bedroom. I could hear his footsteps as they got closer to my bedroom. And then his voice.

"BOBBY, I'M GOING TO THE GAME. AND DON'T YOU LEAVE THIS HOUSE, YOU HEAR ME!"

"Yes...Yes Sir." I said. I could hardly talk. Did I hear him right? Surely he didn't mean......

Daddy got into his car and drove to the game.

I went and sat on the front porch.

I thought to myself...Dad is coming back for me any moment. He is just holding out to punish me. He is making sure I remember how it feels. Surely, he is not going to ignore Mr. Nixon and all the teachers. Surely, he is not going to let all of his men friends down who were probably betting on the game. Surely, he was going to let me play in this game!

....

Well, that memorable event took place over forty-six years ago. And I've never forgotten the lesson that I learned.

I've had many opportunities to remember that day. I've spoken to hundreds of youth during my teaching,

143

counseling and rehabilitation career, often using "that experience" as a reference and I continue to do so.

My Daddy says what he means and means what he says. I disobeyed my Dad and I had to "pay the price for disobedience."

Chapter 18

A Real Man Is A Responsible Man

I've just about concluded my writings and now my sons, Ray, Robert, Rodriquez and Randal have a little information which can help then to understand what the times were like back in the old days before television, spaceships, instant coffee, McDonalds and Kentucky Fried Chicken.

I have only one more chapter to write and it's the most important since each of you are grown men and each of you have children of your own and each of you have a male child.

The summer before my senior year in high school is when this story begins...All summer I had been having a good time. I mean since school was over in June, I had been doing my chores around the house cooking breakfast for Daddy, Billy, and Elaine and going to the Harder Hall or Kenilworth Golf Course to caddie. (Mother still in college) Sometimes I would caddie a single bag for nine holes for $3.00 or eighteen holes for $6.00 or $6.50 with tips. But the best money was carrying double bags, which went for $10.00 for nine holes or $20.00 for eighteen holes. "Wow", $20.00 for about four hours of walking was very good money to make in 1954, 55, & 56.

"Bobby, you going to the golf course today?" asked Billy.

"Naw, I think I'll ride down to Dinner Lake...see if I can't catch a bass or two."

"Don't forget it's your turn to iron the clothes this afternoon." That's my sister, Elaine. She will wash clothes most of the day and it's my turn to iron sheets, pillow cases, pants, shirts, and handkerchiefs. Mother had taught all of us not only how to iron, but we knew how to cook, sew buttons, clean house, etc. Whatever a woman could do, Mother taught us boys to do also. She would say, "In case you boys don't have a wife, you will know how to keep house for yourselves." (Years later I certainly appreciate everything that Mother had taught us.)

"Billy, you wanna ride down to the lake and fish?"

"No way, Bobby. I got to write some more letters to see if I can get into college...somebody got to give me some money; I know there's gotta be some scholarship money somewhere."

Billy worked at the colored theater showing movies during the night and he had been saving money for nearly two years, determined to go to Tuskegee College in Alabama. I hadn't thought much about college. I knew that I was pretty good in football and basketball and whenever I would "day dream" about college I would imagine myself at Florida A. & M. with Coach Jake Gaither playing right halfback for the mighty Florida Rattlers. They had not lost a football game in five years. They were the best colored, college, football team in the nation.

I drove down to Dinner Lake in my 1948 Pontiac. Earlier in the year Dad and I had finally decided that it was best for me to have a car of my own instead of me using his car, and always leaving the gas tank empty. He gave me the Pontiac and bought himself a 1948 Chevrolet. My best friend, Alfred Cooper, also had a green 1948 Pontiac. We kept our cars clean and polished all the time and, of course, we got all the girls and were the envy of all the boys in E. O. Douglas High School.

As I look back to that particular day, I don't remember ever catching any fish. In fact, I recall taking a swim at the colored beach area and just drying off by lying on the long wooden dock.

I remember that day because it was later that evening that my Dad had a long talk with me...and from that moment on I would not have the leisure time of just lying around all summer long doing nothing in particular.

Before I get to that evening talk with Dad, I need to mention that I was dating several girls in school. I had a girl friend in Lake Placid, Avon Park, Lake Wales, Arcadia, Waverly, Haines City and several girl friends who lived in Sebring.

Margie Speakman was my main girl friend. Margie was in the ninth grade and was a very good basketball player. In fact, that is how I met her by traveling on the bus together going to out-of-town basketball games. We usually would sit together on the bus and share our lunches together.

Margie's parents, Black Boy and Mae Hosie Speakman, were good down-to-earth people. When I went to them and asked to date Margie they reminded me of the time to have Margie home during school days by 8 P.M. and 10 P.M. on Friday and Saturday nights. No excuses. In fact, there were many weekends and through the weeks that dates were "carried out" on the front porch in full view of one or both of the parents.

And so, as nature will have its way, Margie and I discovered ways and places to be alone, together. It just so happened that during one of those times in a moment of passion, a baby was conceived.

Many times Dad had spoken to me about being careful with the girls I was seeing. Dad would even leave contraceptives on my bedroom nightstand.

During the 50's it was not proper to talk openly about birth control, and the "pill" had not been developed. "Aids" was not a threatening disease but other forms of venereal diseases were prevalent and I took precautions the majority of the times I was being promiscuous. It just so happened that I got careless on a particular moonlight evening when

Robert J. Walker (Bobby)

Margie and I were parked under the "old Oak tree" at E. O. Douglas High School on the hill.

Getting back to that conversation with my Dad. "Bobby, I wanna talk with you. Come on out to the front porch."

I knew that something serious was about to be said...years ago, Billy and I had learned to watch Dad's face for certain expressions, which were signs of what mood he was in. A smooth forehead without wrinkles was a good mood, when he was whistling and singing, he was an in excellent happy mood. Wrinkles on his forehead and low deep voice tone meant TROUBLE...I WAS IN BIG TROUBLE!

"Black Boy and Mrs. Hosie came to see me today; they wanta know what you gonna do 'bout Margie" I knew what Dad meant 'cause Margie had been acting kinda funny for several weeks...she was throwing up early in the morning, and she hadn't been herself. When we went riding or when we would go over to Avon Park movie theater. (We had a colored movie house in Sebring but the theater in Avon Park was a white theater. They showed new releases and sold "fresh popcorn", but colored folks were allowed to sit only in the balcony.)

We would get these huge bags of popcorn for five cents and Margie would "throw-up." Therefore, I had an idea that Margie was pregnant. She wouldn't say anything to me and I was afraid to bring the subject up to her. Therefore, we just tried to act dumb, thinking "this thing would just go away." It didn't.

I looked Dad straight in the eye and said, "I don't know what to do, but I want to do the right thing...guess I'll have to marry her, right?"

Dad said, "You done done what grown men normally do. Now you got to be a real man and take responsibility for what you done...You got to get a job and take care of that baby, starting right now."

Well, from that day on, my high school life changed. Taking on a real man's responsibilities meant giving up fun in the sun, no more joy riding to Lake Wales, Arcadia, Lakeland, or even Avon Park. No more all day fishing trips, or going hunting "around the wire" or out on Arbuckle Creek Ranch...no more "hanging out" on Lemon

Street drinking strawberry sodas at Bill Robertson's Service Station at night.

I started working with Dad the very next day, cutting white folk's lawns, cutting down trees, raking leaves, and trimming hedges.

When school started in September I took over my brother's old job operating the movie projector at the colored Movie Theater on Highlands Avenue. (My brother, Billy, managed to get enrolled at Tuskegee College.) Whatever money I made working I gave all of it to Dad. I didn't trust myself to keep all that money, neither did my Dad. Therefore, each payday I would give Dad my money, and he would give money to Mae Hosie or Black Boy. When school started I also worked with Dad mowing lawns on Saturdays and holidays...work, work and more work.

My son, Ray Anthony Walker, was born April 19, 1955 and from that day onward, I learned that to be responsible for some one else's life (a baby's) is truly a very serious matter. Yes, I started to learn that just getting a girl pregnant didn't make you a man, but a real man is a responsible man".

When principal Nixon discovered that I was the father of Margie Speakman's baby I was denied participation in extra-curricula activities in school, which meant that I could no longer play football, basketball, sing in the choir, hold office in NFA or play in the Concert Band.

During my senior year in High School, a time when I should have been enjoying myself to the highest degree as a football star or basketball star, instead, I was working. (I received several letters of "intention" from colleges and universities, also a couple of "invitations" to visit certain black colleges for possible scholarships. But, I couldn't think about college now, I had a son to take care of.)

During my last year in school, I should have been really "living it up", instead I was being a "responsible young man" working and contributing to the care of my son. I was baby sitting, and taking Margie to the store. I was washing diapers and boiling baby bottles.

I graduated from E.O. Douglas High School on June 5, 1956. I can still hear those words spoken on that hot summer evening in 1955, by Charlie Walker, my Dad, saying, "Bobby, now you got to be a real man and take responsibility for what you've done".

Conclusion:

For those who read this book, I sincerely hope you find it pleasurable to read about "The Way Things Were" some forty, fifty, and sixty years ago. Others may read this book and a smile comes to your face as you recall similar situations or experiences.

Then of course, some might remember some exact events as I remember them, and last but not least, some of you may read this book and laugh with disbelief, that such events, places, situations, people and creatures ever existed. But I assure you that it is all true, as I remember "The Way Things Were" so long ago.

Today, Thursday January 4, 2001 is the fourth day of a new millenium and as I conclude this series of short stories, I can't help but reflect to those conversations I had with my mother in the year of 1987.

I think Mother would be proud of me for taking her suggestions and compiling this book. My mother (A. B. Walker) passed in February 1992. She taught in the public school systems for some thirty plus years including E. O. Douglas, Woodlawn, Fred Wild and several schools in Georgia. She was known, loved, and respected throughout the state of Florida as a Christian, Humanitarian and an individual who loved people. Nobody was a stranger at her door and everybody got a meal at her table, whether it be man, woman or child, or dog, cat or bird.

Dad (Charlie Walker) continues to reside in Sebring, Florida. We live in the same house that he built in 1944. It has been remodeled with several rooms added: a TV day room, additional car garage, screened patio, tool shed, sewing room, wash room and a small work shed for Dad's "Small Engine Repairs" business. At ninety years of age, Dad continues to work part time with my son, Robert J. Walker, Jr.

My brother, Billy (Col. Charles Walker) graduated from Tuskegee College in 1958. He became an officer in the U. S. Air Force. He completed two Vietnam duty tours flying jets and helicopters. Having been downed twice and wounded in combat, he received The Purple Heart and retired as a Lt. Col. in 1982.

He is married and has six children and is presently residing in Panama City, Florida, where he has taught junior R.O.T.C. at Bay High School for the last fifteen years.

My sister, "Chicken" (Ethel Elaine Walker) has retired and recently moved to Sebring Fla. She is graduate of E.O. Douglas H.S.

She was elected Miss E. O. Douglas in 1958 and taught school here in Highlands County from 1962 – 1965. She has two children and two grandchildren and has a beautiful home on Lake Jackson and She is enjoying her well deserved retirement.

Well, that's exactly what I've done, retired in 1998 and returned to live in Sebring, Florida after twenty-three years working with the Florida Department of Corrections and six years as a superintendent with the Department of Juvenile Justice, prior to working for the State of Florida. I was YMCA director for six years and a Pennsylvania State Labor Coordinator for one year.

I have always held "special memories" of Sebring in my mind and a special "love" in my heart. All the years that I lived away from this small Central Florida City, I remembered the smelling of the citrus trees blooming, the "snowbirds" returning each winter to play golf and fish…the excitement of seeing the colorfully dressed men and women who came each March for the Sebring Endurance Race, the roaring, barooming, zooming sounds of the Austin Healys, BMWs, Triumps, Fiats, Jaguar's and the Ferrari's as they raced up Kenilworth Boulevard going to the Air Field for the race.

Yes, I've always wanted to come back to Sebring and spend time with my dad. I also wanted to return in order to give back in some way to the community and citizens of this "great city".

I realize that many of the people to whom I owe so much, and those who "helped me" and were "kind and fair" with me, are deceased. But I remember people like "Judge" Piety and family, Bossie and Tresa Watson, The Kahn Family of Kahn's Department Store, Mr. and & Mrs. Gilbert of Gilbert's Drug Store, Dr. Martin, Mr. Elli Robertson and oh, so many, many more.

I look back on those childhood years of 1944 –1956, those times, those experiences and now I realize that

"Segregation" was a "Terrible Idea put into practice", a "Bad habit", an "Unjustifiable Fear", a "Misplaced Value", a "Waste of Money, Resources, Potential," a "Loss of Self Worth and Self Integrity".

But, thanks to Father God Almighty, I survived along with many of my Black brothers and sisters, also with many of my White brothers and sisters. "Yes, thank God we all survived" and now we have arrived into a new age, a new time, and a new way from that era.

We can now join hands, hearts, ideas, theories, visions and go forth into in a new millenium, "The WAY THINGS WILL BE!"

The End

Short Biography of
The Reverend Robert Walker
Sebring, Florida

Born August 7, 1938 in Macon, Georgia, Walker attended E. O. Douglas School in Sebring and spent two years in the Air Force.

In Tuskegee University, he received a BS degree in Administration and a MS degree from Springfield University in Massachusetts and was certified in YMCA work.

He was an ordained minister in the Greater Bethel Primitive Baptist Church and is a certified counselor.

He was employed by the Florida Department of Corrections, was a prison superintendent and the Department of Juvenile Justice in Lantana, Florida.

Walker was ordained in 1996 in the Non-Denominational Redemption Life Fellowship by Harold Ray and is presently associated with the Bountiful Blessing Church of God in Sebring with Bishop Timothy McGahee.

He is currently serving as president of the Highlands County Minority Economic Development Council, Inc.

Walker is married to the former Beatrice Penny Fitzpatrick and has four sons. He retired in 1998 to Sebring to be with his elderly father. At the prompting of his mother in 1987, Walker began writing a series of short stories about growing up in Sebring, Florida.

Printed in the United States
95892LV00005B/22-129/A

9 781403 382283